My Uncle George

ALASTAIR PHILLIPS

My Uncle George

The respectful recollections of a backslider
in a Highland manse

RICHARD DREW PUBLISHING
Glasgow

First published 1984 by
Richard Drew Publishing Ltd
6 Clairmont Gardens, Glasgow G3 7LW
Scotland

Editor: Antony Kamm

Designed by James W Murray

Illustrated by Sally Orr

British Library Cataloguing in Publication Data
Phillips, Alastair
My Uncle George.
1. Caithness – Social life and customs
I. Title
941.16′2082′0924 DA880.C1
ISBN 0-86267-075-6

The publisher acknowledges
subsidy from
The Scottish Arts Council
towards the publication
of this volume

Set in Linotype Cheltenham Book
by John Swain & Son Glasgow Limited
Made and Printed in Great Britain by
Butler & Tanner Ltd, Frome, Somerset

CONTENTS

Introduction, *page* 7

CHAPTER 1 Cows, cabbages and Sunday,

2 Mistress of the manse,

3 The 'Mercies' without comment,

4 Villains and Voluntaries,

5 Uncle George lets me down,

6 In dangerous company,

7 The courtship of Uncle George,

8 A permissive interlude,

9 Hurricanes in the pulpit,

10 The language of Eden,

11 Walking with great men,

12 Travelling occasions,

13 The Macaphee sub-culture,

14 Fun and games,

15 Lewis and more travelling occasions,

16 Discretions of Aunt Maggie,

17 Old and mild,

INTRODUCTION

T H E Uncle George of this nostalgia was the Rev. George Mackay, for 35 years the Free Church of Scotland minister at Fearn, a lush agricultural enclave of Easter Ross. He was, in his turn, Moderator of the General Assembly of that Church. He died in 1944 (while I was in Normandy) and was buried in the churchyard of Fearn Abbey — an ancient religious foundation, but, being now an Auld Kirk, or 'Moderate' establishment, one for which he had evinced more tolerant condescension than outright reverence in his lifetime.

Although the denomination to which he belonged is not large — they are after all the 'Wee' Frees — it is a body with strong and sincere beliefs and outspoken convictions; and it has produced many resolute and commanding personalities of whom, I like to think, Uncle George was a prime example. But he was neither harsh, nor was he as narrow as his fellows have been popularly painted. Uncle George may have been rigid in his views, stern and uncompromising in his attitude on matters of conduct which his Church regarded as fundamental; but he was kind, in many essential ways as frail as the rest of us, and he was a humorous daily companion.

He was born in Lybster, on the seaward side of Caithness, and, himself an only child, was married into a large and individualistic landward tribe of crofting and sheep-rearing Sinclairs, into whose familial affairs he was intimately, if discreetly, drawn. The paths crossed constantly; an interchange in which I partook, so that much of what happened in the manse at Fearn was relevant to the daily life, some sixty miles to the north, on the homestead of Westerdale, to which all the scattered kin returned from time to time.

Dunbeath, latterly also on the circuit, is the coastal parish and practice where my older brother became the general practitioner, and where my mother, the last survivor of her generation, returned to dominate what was left of the family; much in the spirit of my formidable grandmother whom she closely resembled.

These memories had their origin in random pieces which I wrote for the Week-end Page of the Glasgow Herald, and these, expanded to include some of the rest of the family and its adherents, are what follow.

CHAPTER ONE

COWS, CABBAGES AND SUNDAY

THE most affectionate recollection I have of my Uncle
George is of him pacing with *Sartor Resartus* open in his hand,
between the stable door and the henhouse, supervising myself as I
wrought with a muck-hoe to scrape long splashes of cow dung off the
newly whitewashed gable end of the byre.

We were both labouring under a certain amount of protest. I had
made my gesture carelessly, and was paying for it. He was standing
guard when he would much rather have been at the bottom of the
garden, with his carbolic cloth in his hand, watching progress in his
favourite bee-hive — the one labelled Sustentation Fund.

He was, however, resigned to the duty, and when every now and
again my aunt looked out to see that neither of us had deserted, and
took the opportunity of improving on the verbal row to which I had
already submitted, he would look up from the book, and, pausing in
the patrol, his fingers in the place, say, 'Calm yourself, Maggie.'

There were three tasks which I abominated. In their order of merit
they were cleaning out the henhouse, weeding the gravel path with a
dutch hoe, and mucking the byre. I did all of them regularly and badly
and in a surly temper. On this day I was sent to muck the byre when I
wanted to be fishing on Loch Eye. The byre was Augean, the graip was
mislaid, and the great shovel was so heavy with caked manure that I
could not use it. To dislodge this accumulation I dragged the shovel
sulkily behind me and beat it against the corner of the byre wall. The

9

first blow was effective and that was what put on the whitewash the marks which I was now under orders to remove.

Uncle George could be very tolerant and understanding when I had offended only against the domestic rules and regulations imposed impartially upon us by Aunt Maggie. And for this present sympathy I readily, if temporarily, forgave him the ebony walking-stick with the silver and bone handle with which from time to time he impressed upon me the wisdom of keeping the Sabbath day, for even then I was a backslider and thought more of Sexton Blake than of the first chapter of the *Life of David Livingstone,* which in ten and more years of summer holidays was as far as I ever got with my approved Sunday reading.

The auto-da-fé was not always entirely spiritual, but sometimes included a suggestion of temporal correction. Uncle George was deeply versed in the identification of the acts of necessity and mercy, among which he included the immediate punishment of breaches of the Sabbath. While this spared me the distress of waiting till Monday, it had some other disadvantages.

There was for example, a fine Sunday morning in July about the end of the First World War. The door of the hayloft faced south and took the best of the sun. I was basking there with the ladder pulled up after me and so transported by a Dixon Hawke that I did not hear the call to prayer when it came time to set out for the church. They looked for me and found me, with the damnable book — such literature was generally condemned under the title of 'no-vells'.

Uncle George took the stick from the hall-stand and dealt with me as a sinner, then hurried off to suck two raw eggs in the vestry and give the Gaelic congregation the benefit of the rest of his indignation. Aunt Maggie lingered to skelp my ears for ripping my best Sunday trousers when scrambling from the loft, and to repair the damage once Uncle George was safely out of sight. Sewing, even in the interests of decency, was not included in his catalogue of the acts of necessity and mercy. 'Don't tell your uncle,' she said as we set out after him to sit and sing loudly and sleep quietly in the manse pew, where, in the convention of the Free Church, we stood to pray and sat to sing.

We sang, of course, without instrumental assistance, following as best we could Johnny Urquhart, the precentor, who always led the praise at a pitch beyond his own register and unattainable by all but the three strongest sopranos in the congregation, of whom Aunt Maggie was one.

She was a credit to the manse, because from long training at family worship and in the catechising which had been an ordinance in my grandfather's house, she knew the words of all the Psalms and sang them with her eyes shut.

I used to think that it was that tight squeezing of the eyelids that helped her to reach the high notes quicker and hold them longer than the woman from Hilton who was her nearest rival. I was proud of her and felt again every Sunday that she earned the sleep which she took with a dignity that looked like profound attention during the discourse. There was no need to feel sorry for the runner-up. She had her regular hour of strident triumph during the week at the Gaelic prayer-meeting which the minister's wife did not attend.

I used to sleep a little myself with my arms folded and my head on the bookboard, but never very soundly, for the cushion on the manse pew was thin and shifting position was a complicated movement and one which it was difficult to carry out unobtrusively because my legs were too short to reach the floor.

I did not even doze that Sunday for I was smarting both top and bottom. Instead I wore my sanctimonious and devout mask, and every time Uncle George, who was a restless preacher, strode to our side of the wide pulpit, I caught his eye and tried to look as if I understood what he was saying about Sanctification and Justification.

I might have spared myself my unctuousness, for when we got back to the manse we found that the garden gate had been left open, and the cow had got in and eaten most of the cabbages and trampled the rest into the ground. She had also had a feed of green peas, and was swelled up like a balloon. We had to send for the vet to come and puncture her side to let the gas off.

'That,' said Uncle George, when the crisis had, as one might say, blown over, 'is a judgment on us for your reading that trashy no-vell in the loft this morning,' and he went again for the ebony stick. By that time, I felt, he was beginning to brood about the cabbages, to which he was partial, as well as about the sin.

It's a funny thing about that walking-stick: I can remember it so well; I can see it, as if it was in my own hall-stand, with its cross handle, and its silver ferrule. The emblem of correction. But I cannot remember any of its strokes. There are no weals; and I doubt now if there ever were any. It was probably more flourished than applied.

Yet it endures as a sanction and a threat. Nor was it one that I always accepted meekly. Indeed to the end, though I had long forgotten it, Uncle George used to recall with relish one such occasion when, smarting, but holding the tears back, I defied him in the name of my absent father, saying:

'Just you wait till I tell him, when he will break your stick and throw you on the dung-heap' — a final resting-place with which I had some obsession by reason of the amount of byre-mucking which at that time seemed to be my lot.

The threat of course, as we both knew, was totally empty, for though my father topped Uncle George by a good six inches, he was the most pacific of men, never given to lifting his hand even to the likes of myself. He was always content to hear that, when I deserved it, as I usually did, I had been skelped at school.

As a matter of fact the only activist, the only basically aggressive person, on that side of the family was my paternal Aunt Caroline, who revelled in being one of the more vigorous and inventive of her generation of suffragettes in Aberdeen.

She was a concert pianist of some celebrity, whose sensitive hands had been known more than once to pour noxious substances into pillar-boxes. And on occasion she had chained herself to railings, to the embarrassment of her brother who, as a journalist in the same town, had occasion to report what he could not avoid seeing.

And it was from Aunt Carrie, in the reminiscent mood which never deserted her, that I learned (though I swear that I never practised it) the technique of silent shop-window-breaking at night, with brown paper, treacle, and a boiler-maker's hammer.

The ploy of which Aunt Carrie was proudest — not for its non-violence but for its insolence and organisation — was the one when she and a raiding party of like-minded feminists, intruded under cover of darkness into the policies of Balmoral Castle when the Monarch was in residence, and replaced all the flags in the holes in the putting green with others bearing the legend 'Votes for Women'.

She was also an early Socialist, and a buddy of Ramsay Macdonald in the days before he succumbed to the seductions of being a social lion.

I do not know if Aunt Carrie ever met Uncle George, but I doubt if she ever did; for it would certainly have been the purpose of the rest of the family, on both sides, to keep them apart. She was a dedicated rationalist, her closest friends were Unitarians, and it always amazed her that her brother, easy-going as he might be in his own observances, had united himself to a tribe of contumacious Caithness Free Presbyterians.

To round off Aunt Carrie — who, as must be obvious, has no part in the Highland traditions and devotions with which I am immediately concerned — she was the first woman journalist on the staff of the Aberdeen Journal, she would fight with her shadow, and she was a very good pianist.

It is a long parenthesis from the ebony walking-stick to Aunt Carrie. The immediate discipline of the manse resided in the back of Aunt Maggie's hand, which she applied without recriminations, and plainly without ill-will. With the exception of some scriptural matters which she took in her stride, the management of the establishment lay entirely in her hands, and when I fell by the wayside, as in the use of certain words which I may have picked up in the adjacent farms steadings, she never said, 'I'll tell your Uncle.' She left these things for him to find out by himself.

It is one of my most affectionate memories of Aunt Maggie that she was never a clype. Maybe that's because she had too many brothers of her own.

CHAPTER TWO

MISTRESS OF THE MANSE

IN my essentially secular recollections of a Highland
manse I do not see Uncle George so much other-worldly as having no
head for business. A benefactress once left a legacy which produced
an annual sum of £25 to be distributed among the poor of the fishing
villages of Hilton and Balintore. The money came to the minister, who
had complete discretion in its disposal.

Uncle George used to take it in his pocket and, starting at the north
end of the village, would pay it out where he thought it was most
needed. This led to a great deal of grumbling and even to hints of
misappropriation, because in his hands the alms were all gone by the
time he had visited half-a-dozen homes. The protests at last so
distressed him that he put the duty on Aunt Maggie, who had a much
better idea of the value of money.

She turned the legacy into shillings and florins, and spread it evenly
through the whole length of the villages, but in such small sums that
none of the beneficiaries was satisfied and she earned a reputation for
meanness that she did not deserve.

She was thrifty, as she needed to be, and she made the minimum
stipend go a long way. She looked at finance with cautious
confidence, believing that between the Lord and herself, in both of
whom she had implicit faith, 'We will be taken honourably through.'

Invaluable small supplements to the stipend came from the natural
and regular increase of her cow. In the summer time I seem to

14

recollect that there was always a bull-calf being hand-fed in the croquet green, where the grass was seldom less than a foot high and where I never saw a hoop. There never seemed to be heifers. It was one of Uncle George's diversions to teach the bull-calves to box. He was never seriously discouraged, because the calves were always sold before they were big enough to be more dangerous than playful.

I was once alone in the manse — Uncle George and Aunt Maggie were off to the communion at Lairg — when the cow gave birth to twins. I was much more alarmed about it than the cow — that would be Bessie — and took so long to run for the Balmuchy cattleman that by the time he arrived all three were on their feet and doing well.

I did, however, feel a little mystified when Aunt Maggie's first orders on her return home some hours later were to banish me from the byre. Even in my innocence I had a feeling that she was a little too late.

—— * ——

Aunt Maggie, as I have hinted, was thrifty. This was necessary in one who had to make do on the stipend of a Free Church minister, and with her thrift went a deep sense of the importance of keeping up appearances. Whatever economies were practised behind the scenes — and many of these were, to say the least, ingenious — she contrived always to present a prosperous front even to the unexpected visitor. She was steadfast in resisting the patronage of the wives of the wealthy farmers with whom Easter Ross surrounded her. This was a necessary part of her faith that in all things, and mainly in those financial, she would 'be taken honourably through'.

The manse was often in the way of receiving gifts from the gardens and fields of the congregation. But when Aunt Maggie accepted a sack of potatoes or a basket of gooseberries it was the giver who felt privileged. She had an unreserved contempt for those through-ither housekeepers among ministers' wives who allowed themselves to show what she called 'a poor mouth'.

Sometimes among ourselves we lunched off potatoes and milk and scones in the morning room, but at Communion when the manse was full of visitors, and two of the spare leaves were in the dining room table, there was always a salmon, and a handsome hospitality. She had this talent for being equal to the occasion from her father, my grandfather, who was a great provider, and prepared for the Communion at Westerdale by having the platform brought across the road from the school and erected on trestles in what in his house was called the pass-room. There it was laid as a table and loaded, and from the fast day to the men's day it fed all who were hungry — kin, preacher, 'the Good Men', and the strangers that the children were sent to bring in from the dykeside.

Aunt Maggie came from a generation and a country that did not know the baker's van. In my grandfather's house 'loaf-bread' was a luxury which was brought at the end of market days from Thurso. The first morning duty of the housewife after she had stirred up the rested peat fire in the open hearth was to put on the girdle and do the baking.

The kist along the back wall of the low kitchen was divided in three, and held, packed so tight that they had to be dug out with a knife, flour, oatmeal, and barley meal. The treacle barrel was in an outhouse. And from these came every morning white scones and treacle scones and barley scones, and bannocks, a foot across and a quarter of an inch thick, which curled when they were set up on their edges round the red peats.

The custom survived in the manse, though the van came often and there was a baker in the village.

Our cousins in Tain were more sophisticated, and I always had the impression that to them there was a certain cachet in having a fancy baker within three minutes walk of the house, to supply on demand loaf-bread, tea-bread, French cakes, and German biscuits.

One of them in many ways resembled Aunt Maggie. Indeed at some points their temperaments were so similar that when they came into conflict they spoke out rather more pointedly than the rest of us did. I remember once she was with us for the better part of a week at the manse. She was a critical guest and easily offended. Her opinion of the manse cuisine was given expression in the course of one of those disputes in which women, finding the original point at issue inadequate to sustain all their indignation, send their minds scouting for additional subjects for caustic remark. This is called 'casting-up'.

That time our cousin, surely with a Tain baker's window in her mind's eye, closed the argument with the scathing and irrelevant comment, 'Scones, scones, nothing but scones.'

This, I thought, was unjust, for under Aunt Maggie's management we ate well and her scones, varied, plentiful, and filling, were but the bulk in a menu which frequently included such gooseberry tart as one can remember for thirty years.

There were, however, others who did not appreciate her true generosity and the high moral sense that made her sympathetic towards poverty but censorious of begging. When a tramp came to the door and said he was hungry she fed him. Some clearly felt that she took them too literally at their word.

Once when she was at home in Westerdale a big strong tinker came to the kitchen door. On those holiday visits she was in the habit of reassuming many of the housekeeping responsibilities that, as an elder daughter, she had conducted with great efficiency before her marriage.

The tinker's opening gambit was to make the traditional poor mouth. Aunt Maggie waited for no more, but, leaving him on the doorstep, went into the kitchen. Within two minutes she was back with an enormous buttered oatmeal bannock in her hands. Gracious and compassionate, she said, 'Have you a pocket?'

'Aye,' said the cyard, as he turned to seek more acceptable alms at the next house along the road, 'but no' for that.'

She never got on very well with the tinkers. They seemed to sense her disapproval of their idleness. There was a black-avised woman who came to the door once when I was in the background. She was pretending to sell cups and saucers, but, naturally, expected to be given something more than their market price. That was not Aunt Maggie's way. She drove an honest but hard bargain. On the minimum stipend and with a fifteen-room manse to maintain in decency you must insist on seeing your money's worth.

Aunt Maggie did not manage to get the last word in that encounter. They had haggled for some minutes when the tinker, seeing that she had met her match, turned away, saying:

'You can kiss my airse.'

As she turned, the shawl she wore round her shoulders parted at the back and a small face as brown as her own peered over the fringe of the plaid and gave the *nunc dimittis*:

'And ye can kiss mine tae.'

The Caithness tinkers never lack an answer. They may seem primitive and sometimes wild in their behaviour when they have been drinking and forget to whine, but it should not be assumed that culture has passed them by.

I was standing with Aunt Maggie one day in my cousin's store when some of the local tribe came trailing along the road from Glutt, and halted their spring cart for long enough to come in and ask for a bit of tobacco. There were half-a-dozen of them, including a remarkably vivid child of about four years. She was the colour of mahogany with a sharp intelligent face and piercing bold black eyes. Her hair, matted and hung with peat meals and soot from the last camping place, was blue black. While her adult relations were whimpering over the counter she stood looking innocently at them with her arm up to the elbow in a biscuit tin that was standing on a box by the door.

Aunt Maggie, seduced from taking notice of the stealing by the personality of the child, patted her on the head and said, 'And what is your name?'

The answer came back like a stoat out of a dyke, 'Shirley Temple Macaphee.'

Aunt Maggie, from her earliest years, believed it her duty to encourage industry in others. As a grown-up daughter in a large family she had excellent opportunities for fulfilling her mission. Her younger brothers and sisters learned to be wary, and I have heard my mother say that for years they never thought of going past the Westerdale kitchen window except on hands and knees. To forget and raise the head was to be buttonholed and set to washing dishes or bringing in peats from the stack.

In my day the burden was the pump. The water supply to the manse at Fearn came from a spring in the middle of the glebe, and was piped to a huge tank in the roof. On the wall of the washing house behind the kitchen there was a pump. It had a wooden handle, polished with years of use. Once the water started drawing it grew heavy, and to fill the tank you had to saw it back and fore for an hour. It was a task that imposed its own discipline, for if one grew lazy and paused for a breather the water ran back in the pipe and it took five minutes of violent pumping before it started to flow again.

The only thing to do was to take it slowly and steadily and devise mental exercises to break the tedium of the labour. Thus, mounted on a chair, for I was too small to reach the handle from the floor, I would count the strokes like a change-ringer, going from one to twelve and back again and then introducing variations to the limit of my arithmetic, such as counting in odd numbers and even numbers. You could vary the number of beats taken with each hand and keep a tally on the wall with a bit of chalk. I even tried reading, but that was never successful.

Any way I took it, it was a labour, less 'fousome', but more regular than mucking the byre or digging the guano out of the henhouse. I sometimes dodged the duty, but not often, for Aunt Maggie had a sharp eye and a good understanding of evasion. Many a time I had reached the gate on my way to a tryst with the cattleman's son and a ferret at Balmuchy, and thought myself safe, when that same soprano that dominated the praise in the church recalled me from the back door with the single cry which I never dared ignore, 'Alastair, the pump.'

Aunt Maggie also made us weed the walks and turn the hay in the open space round the church, but that was a combined operation which had not the loneliness and feeling of endlessness of the stint at the pump.

Unlike the lion's young, which hungry be, we never lacked our food. There was always plenty, but no waste, and Aunt Maggie was an artist with the mincer. She was herself fond of her food, though she liked to complain of a dainty stomach. But being practical, she was able to satisfy both her healthy appetite and her gratification in being dyspeptic. She went the full course with relish and counteracted it with an immediate draught of health salts, which came to the table in its tin with the cruet.

She was skilful in her economies, which were employed within the framework of her rules for keeping up appearances. Some were more effective than others. Some failed from the irresponsibility of the servant-girl. The kitchen stove was a finely balanced example of calculated economy. It was possible to bring the flues to a state of congestion at which the draught was so gentle that there was no wastage of coal. This never lasted for more than a few days, because the girl, once Aunt Maggie's back was turned, was sure to lay on so hard with the bellows that she put the chimney on fire and dissipated all the hainingly accumulated soot. This was so much the common order that it was accepted with resignation; and if, when driving over the hill towards Cadboll, Aunt Maggie looked back and saw a pall of smoke on the sky-line, she would just say, 'That girl,' and drive on.

When I took to authorised smoking she was not displeased. Uncle George and all her brothers were heavy smokers, and she saw it as quite the proper thing in a young man. But she did not think much of those expensive cigarette things.

'What you'll chust do,' she advised me, 'is to smoke a pipe like your uncle. And you'll buy bogey roll. Take you the ounce of it and cut it up all at one time, and rub it down fine with your hands and put it in your tobacco pouch. Then nobody will know the difference.'

—— * ——

Aunt Maggie was the best administrator I have ever known. True she did not talk the jargon of modern economics, but if Chancellors of the Exchequer knew as much as she did about liquidity, the balance of payments would be the least of our national problems.

I never knew, for it never occurred to me to inquire, what my uncle's stipend amounted to, but there is no doubt that it had not much improved since the hey-day of Sweet Auburn, when the incumbent was passing rich on forty pounds a year. And so there was an undoubted genius who presided over the unremitting exercise of making ends meet in a twelve-roomed manse. Nay, more. Twelve rooms, nearly as many 'offices', and a system of outhouses which implied that the minister had the means to run a coach-and-pair, employ a stable-lad, operate a minimal dairy-farm, breed his own bacon, and maintain a poultry hatchery.

While the whole house was spaciously laid out, there were two rooms, large, handsomely furnished (by Whittock and Reid of Edinburgh, the gift of a prosperous adherent and family connection), ritually dusted and special, and not for the daily intercourse of the family; who breakfasted and dined in the morning room, and relaxed either in the study — if a sermon was not in preparation, or elsewhere, usually the kitchen.

The drawing room and dining room had keys turned in their doors, to discourage casual visitation and the consequent blemish of muddy or sharny footmarks on the pale carpets, or the inevitable greasy finger- or palmprints upon the polished surfaces.

When I was admitted to these sanctuaries (for indeed they awed me at the time as holy places), it was when I was washed, properly dressed and on my best behaviour. That was when the manse was full of assisting divines for the Communion; or when Aunt Maggie was giving afternoon tea to those wives of the local affluence before whom she owed it to herself to keep the flag flying. Farming in Easter Ross had done splendiferously in the First World War, a prosperity that tended to give the farmers' wives a certain hauteur.

But Aunt Maggie never let the side down, and when the dining room door was open, the table, with its two extra leaves added, groaned and the silver gleamed. She inherited that capacity from my grandfather, 'the great provider'. There were, of course, subventions for these great occasions, from not exactly secret, but just discreet sources. Nothing furnished a table more suitably to help the sharp appetites of a convocation of Highland ministers than the whole boiled salmon on

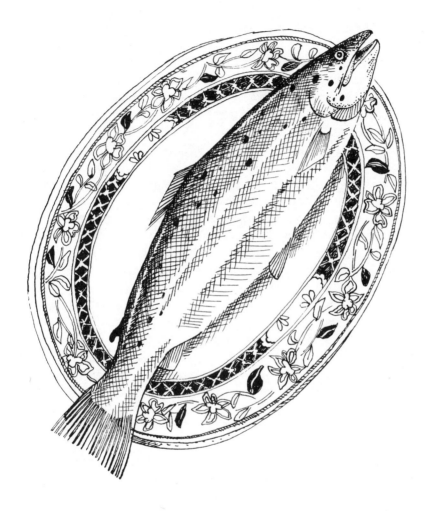

a lordly dish. And as for the game in season (or out of it for that matter) the only requirement was that, if complimented on the repast, the minister himself should remain a little absent-minded, other-worldly and incurious.

The lay-out of the manse was spacious, with a big, square red-tiled hall, surrounded by a staircase and gallery. But I remember even better the long dark passage leading to the morning-room and kitchen quarters. It was on a narrow table there that the oil lamps were daily trimmed and filled. And even now I just need to take a sniff through the nose to be again splashing in the paraffin while trying to direct it out of its surging into the inadequate little funnels, which always sat askew in the lamp-bowls. This was because when you unscrewed the burner and the globe, laughably in order not to make a mess, you had to leave the wicks dangling in the bowl. This meant that the burner had to be held high in the left hand, while with the right hand only, you had to manhandle the oil can, and direct the stream of paraffin into the wobbling tin funnel. To do this cleanly was patently a two-person job; but the manse was always short-staffed. Indeed after the stable-lad enlisted and went off, with the horse, to the First World War, the establishment consisted of ourselves and one maid, who had plenty else to do.

There will not be so many folk nowadays who will be remembering just how vulnerable lamp-glasses were. It was not so much that they slipped out of your hands and shattered, as that badly trimmed wicks blackened them with smoke, and errant flames brought them out in cracks and holes at their bulbous part. Cleaning the soot out of the inside of a cracked lamp glass was a delicate and tricky operation, but economy required that it had to be attempted. New lamp-glasses were luxuries reserved for the best standard lamps in the more or less public apartments. For the rest it was make-do and mend, an operation for which the essential material was the sticky flaps of cheap envelopes, which were stuck over the holes in the globes, and gradually — or not so gradually — were incinerated. So that my abiding recollection of the domestic lighting of the manse is the smell of paraffin and burnt paper.

That we never lacked our food, nor indeed our simple luxuries, was thanks in some degree to a self-sufficient trading practice. This was the barter system which went into operation when the grocer's van came twice a week and the eggs of our free-running hens were turned into loaf-bread, and jam, and tea, and other essentials.

I have no idea what the overall rate of exchange was, because I usually remained in the background during these transactions. I was waiting until the coast was clear, so that I could make my own private bargain. Not that we haggled, for it had long been settled between me and the vanman that the going rate for the four eggs that I always had concealed on my person was one small packet of Mitchell's Prize Crop cigarettes. The beauty about free-running hens is that they lay away.

On some occasions, when the craving was irresistible I might lie with my head in my bedroom fender and blow the smoke up the chimney; but generally I concealed the packet and indulged the habit perilously in the security of the hayloft with the ladder pulled up. Fortunately I never set anything on fire. That sort of pyrotechnic was adequately and regularly provided by the kitchen chimney.

The hayloft was a fairly safe private retreat where I used to have more or less uninterrupted freedom to consult Sexton Blake and Dixon Hawke and Harry Wharton, whose transactions never had any place on the study bookshelves. Those were the days of the 'Four-pennys', long before D.C. Thomson of Dundee got round to thinking of the *Beano* and the *Dandy*.

—— * ——

There was very much more to my education in the Wee Free manse than the Shorter Catechism and *The Days of the Fathers in Ross-shire*; though for this catholic instruction my classroom was the kitchen and the byre rather than the study. My favourite seat was the hard chair against the wall at the end of the kitchen table where I absorbed current local scandal and old folklore (not all of which I totally understood) while the maid, talking non-stop with a freedom of which I doubt Aunt Maggie would have approved, went about her tasks.

Thus I learned that if a new-wed man had a longing for strong sons he must put a handful of fence-wire staples under the pillow of his marriage-bed.

And, while it was Granny's protection against the evil eye to give me a drink of 'water off silver', it was the Free Church manse servant girl who taught me the immediate first aid of spitting through my crossed fingers every time I might meet a cross-eyed woman.

There were the other little snippets of indisputable country wisdom like 'A hairy man's a happy man; a hairy woman's a witch.' They were mostly landward girls from the neighbouring farms who came to help at the manse, and they never made much of the superstitions about the ill chance of fishermen who met the minister on the way to their boat. But they made much of the magical powers that were woven into harvest knots and corn-dollies. It was from them that I heard my first whispered hint of the fearsome initiation rituals of the Horseman's Word, a subject which I pursued in later years among the hard-headed ploughmen of Aberdeenshire, even to the point of being confided the word, which guaranteed total dominion equally over horses and women: a word, incidentally, which I was sworn never to 'write, recite or indite' on pain of satanic execution.

On the cultural side, the kitchen was rich in folk-song, mostly of the melancholy kind. But while I reacted sentimentally enough to 'O Will Ye Go Luv and Leave me Noo', I really paid more attentive interest to that much longer ballad about the reassurances offered to the husband returning each night to find unfamiliar articles of clothing lurking about the house . . . like the gentleman's overcoat hanging on the kitchen door. A line or two of the refrain will suggest the rare quality of the song, 'O wife, good wife, what's this I see?', etc.

Oh husband dear. . . .
It's nothing but a blanket
My Mother sent to me
(*Reply*) A thousand miles I've travelled,
A thousand miles and more,
But It's buttons on a blanket
I've never seen afore.

I must, however, absolve the chanteuses of the manse kitchen of any responsibility for my subsequent command of all the authentic verses of *The Ball of Kirriemuir*.

There was, however another important aspect to the singing that I heard in the kitchen. At first I thought it was excellently unseemly and risky to hear Bessie humming one of the venerated Psalm tunes, and then break into unfamiliar, but enchanting words, and trolling:

There was an Auld Seceder cat,
And he was unco grey,
He catched a moose within God's hoose,
Upon the Sabbath Day.
The people all were horrified,
And unto it did say,
'O thou perverted, wicked cat
To break the Sabbath Day. . . .'

Of course I did not report her. And it was years before I learned that she was merely reflecting an old and devout tradition under which, except at formal worship, it was sinful to sing the actual words of the

Psalms; and that for learning, practising, or rehearsing the tune, the proper thing to do was to sing worldly words to it. And, I irresistibly thought of Aunt Maggie's strong soprano when I subsequently heard the other variation:

> The high, high notes of Bangor's praise
> Are unco hard to raise,
> And trying for to reach them gars,
> The lassies burst their stays.

—— * ——

By some standards Aunt Maggie's economies were noteworthy — and she did not lack for nieces who were not blate to recount them. But her sense of duty and of generosity were equally highly developed, and practical.

There was a faithful occasional helper behind the scenes at Communion time. Her name was Dollie Vass, and she lived in the fishing village of Balintore. In her maturity she got married, and I was sent down to the village to deliver her wedding present.

It was a cut-glass jam dish; and when I handed it to her, she held it up, shaking her head affectionately and familiarly at it, and apostrophised it, saying, 'My, oh my! many's the time I've filled ye with cheely.'

My most treasured instructor of those formative years was Bessie Campbell, who sheltered me from the consequences of my little misdemeanours, and regaled me with rather worldlier wisdom than I was likely to pick up at the knee of Uncle George, or Aunt Maggie.

But after several years Bessie left, a shade hastily, to wed the second horseman at the adjacent farm of Pitcairie. Soon after this I arrived at Fearn on my annual summer hadj; and as soon as might be I went to see her in her tied cottage. When I quizzed her about the burdens of motherhood she was perfectly relaxed and forthright as she had always been.

'No bother,' she said, 'When he yells I just stap my briest in his mooth.'

And, the occasion arising at that moment, with a deftness of the wrist that was enchanting to observe, she suited the action to the word. It was a gesture as natural and jocose as the one she had used in the past when I interrupted her while she was milking the cow. Then, with a small twist of the fingers, she would direct a stream of milk straight from the cow's teat to splash into my face at four paces.

CHAPTER THREE

THE 'MERCIES' WITHOUT COMMENT

Round about Communion time always, and oc-
casionally at less ordained seasons during the rest of the year, a fine
bit of salmon would be delivered to the manse. This was fish that the
most saintly of assisting ministers might eat with an easy conscience;
a manna unblemished, about which Aunt Maggie need not fear being
put to the question. Not that the ministers, many of whom had the
same background as ourselves, ever did. Salmon, in the Highlands, is
one of the mercies that is best taken with an uninquisitive appetite.

Communion salmon, at least, came always in legitimate gift from
the fishery at Hilton operated by the Paterson family, who, although
United Frees, held Uncle George in a personal affection, and saw to
it that the sacramental entertainment at the Wee Free manse was
traditional and worthy. Communion without boiled salmon was in-
conceivable.

The Patersons, however, were the only ones whom one might
openly commend for their generosity. Aunt Maggie, who had a sense
of occasion and a private set of rules of fitness, might say, if the guests
included some of the more knowing and notoriously pious, 'This is a
beautiful fish that was sent up from Hilton.'

It always sounded to me, who had a fair idea where the other fish
came from, like a sort of 'All clear'.

There were, you see, other benefactors, as was only to be expected in a family such as ours, which was much given to free fishing in Caithness. They made their gifts without the expectation of any but the most cryptic acknowledgment. There would sometimes come a letter to the manse which, among obvious and innocent gossip, would say, 'If you get a parcel by train, put an X at the end of your letter when you reply.'

The sign was both receipt and thanks.

The train was a more reliable courier than the post, particularly when the sending end was a place where the nearest relatives of the postmistress were gillies. You could go over the hill and stop the south-going train at the Altnabreac Halt, and slip the long, distinctive parcel into the guard's van. Railwaymen, if not incurious, were sympathetic and did not blab.

In this matter of opportune salmon Uncle George was neither narrow-minded nor inquisitive. He did not count poaching among the penible shortcomings which he saw and deplored in his brothers-in-law and nephews. Indeed he was quite sound on the theory of taking salmon with the cleek, though I never came across any direct evidence of his practical acquaintance with the art. Nor did he consider a poaching story unfit for young ears. He was just discreet enough to avoid mentioning names.

He did not frown every time he came through the kitchen door into my grandmother's house at Westerdale, though he knew as well as any of us that the gaff, sharp and handy for any providential run of fish in the river, lay in the gutter above the lintel under which he had to duck his head.

He would, indeed, have been hard-wrought had he been officious

and censorious. As it was, he looked with indulgent shortsightedness past an operation in which he took no active part, and he came contentedly and with a virtuous appetite to the table.

In this way he may have missed some good excitements. For instance . . . .

—— * ——

'They tell me,' remarked the joiner, himself an artist with the three hooks, but a progressive man who would give any innovation a fair try, 'that with the chelignite you can make a prodigious explosion.' My (and Uncle George's) relative, conservative though from ancient custom he was in the habit of voting for Sir Erchie Sinclair, preferred the rod (with a worm) for sport, or the net for the urgent demands of the pot, and was inclined to be sceptical. He asked, 'Would it, think you, be as big as the explosion you can get with a tin of carbide and a hole in each end?'

'The Hydro-electric,' said the joiner, 'makes holes in mountains with it, and I'm thinking that just a wee inchie of it in a pool I know up the strath would maybe turn up an antran fish and save us the bother of carrying that awkward net and looking suspicious.'

The free fisher in the Highlands in recent years has been seriously inconvenienced by the vigilance that has been brought upon the waters by the wholesale methods of the commercial poachers.

In the days of my grandfather, they tell me, the only difference between yourself and the tenant who paid high fees for the upper beats of say, the Thurso River was that you were by heredity and local training the more skeely, and could take with a Stewart tackle the fish that would not look at his Butchers or the fancy flies that he bought from those incomparable confidence men, the gillies.

The biggest fish that ever came out of the Thurso River between Tormsdale and Loch More was landed not by any expensively accoutred sportsman from the South but by the father of the postmistress at Westerdale. That, of course, was an official record, which took no account of the great fish that sometimes yielded without a taste of the hook to the naked gaff.

The authorised fishing in those waters was, if we remember, remarkable for a continuously recurring coincidence. Day after day the fishing tenants, well and obsequiously attended by their gillies, would thrash the water from morning until late afternoon without a bite. Then, wearied with failure, they would call up their coach and be

28

off to the lodge for their tea. And the gillie would see them off, saying, 'I'll just make a last cast or two and then I'll be off home for my denner mysel'.'

But it nearly always happened that no sooner had the party won back to the lodge than the telephone rang, and it would be the gillie reporting, 'You were hardly round the bend of the road when I got into a good fish. I'll be sending it up in a wee while.'

It is the duty of a good gillie to see that his chentlemen do not fail to the point of utter discouragement. And it is wonderful what can be done if you take off the fancy fly and put on a big hook and a handful of worms.

In those days, fishing free or with the blessing of the proprietor, you took your fish one at a time even in the moments of haste and unorthodoxy when you kicked off your trousers and went into the pool after them with a gaff.

One of the most brilliant feats of urgent fishing I can remember was performed by my late Uncle James to remove a piece of damning evidence left in the millpool by three of us, childish and careless cousins. We had gone guddling with a gaff which had lain so long in the sun that the wood had warped and left the head loose in the handle. When we sent for help there was a fish swimming round the pool like a surfacing submarine, the periscope the shining head of the gaff sticking fair out of his back.

In other straths between Helmsdale and the Naver the cleek, still a one-man weapon, was sanctioned by tradition if not by the landlord. This is a fishing that calls for intimate knowledge of the water and three cod hooks whipped back to back on the end of a long line. The tackle is sometimes known as the ripper and is used like a grappling iron. On stretches likely to be overlooked by keepers it may, in the hands of an expert, be manipulated on the end of a line reeling out of an apparently innocent fishing rod.

Then with the increasing market value of the fish came the net and the poison (a shovelful of certain brands of oxygen-excluding fertiliser is said to be deadly) and the high explosive, and the organised raiders who came from towns with fast motor cars; and poaching became a profession and the prevention of it a strategy of total warfare.

These are the unhappy, one might almost say the debauching, circumstances that brought such naturally honest and gentle minds as that of the joiner I mentioned to thoughts of gelignite.

In the remoter parts of the North, gelignite is hard to come by. It must also be inquired after with discretion.

The joiner was stumped but not discouraged. He considered his problem, discovered it to be scientific and chemical, and took it to the doctor, a reliable and proven partner whether after deer or salmon. The doctor, though he had heard that the stuff was unchancy, was not repelled by the idea, and communicated with a former classmate in the South.

After some delay he had, for his inquiry, a plain and heavily wrapped parcel and an anonymous and cryptic covering note saying 'Before you do anything, for God's sake read the instructions on the lid of the box.'

The three of them — the joiner, the roadman and my kinsman, the doctor — had a trial explosion in the sea, where they depth-charged a deep fiord from the top of a high rock. The rock shook a little, but they were delighted with the column of water that came up and drenched them, and were gratified on returning to the village to find that it was being taken for granted and without inquisitiveness that a naval vessel out of Scapa was engaged in gunnery practice somewhere to the north.

In the dusk of the evening they took their box to the pool that they knew of up the strath, a fine and secret place rife with fish, deep and dark and peaty, and concealed from the telescopes of prying keepers within the overhanging sides of a high gorge. A bridge arched above the water and there they prepared the charge and from there they launched it.

Maybe in the darkness they had overloaded the cartridge, maybe they had forgotten that the open sea will absorb and dissipate a detonation more readily than a narrow, rocky funnel. Whatever the reason, they got a terrible fright.

The bridge reeled under them like a see-saw, and when the water that had gone up started to come down on them it was full of stones. The noise, they were sure, would be heard by every river-watcher north of the Highland Line. They did not wait to assess the fishing, but took straightway to the heather and each by his own route, crept home.

But the noise must have gone straight up into the heavens, for no one took note of it, not even the faintly slow-witted shepherd who lived just over the brow of the hill. The explosion did not disturb him, and the following morning when he went as usual to draw two buckets of water from the river he was stricken with a great wonder to see many dead fish floating on its surface.

He liked fish, and he had relatives in Glasgow who liked fish, but he was canny, and he felt that this bounty was not natural. Nor was he one to talk carelessly and lose the harvest. So he went back to the croft and got a sack, and he put four of the biggest fish in it and carried it over the hill to the village.

He was the second patient who was admitted to the doctor's morning surgery. He came in and closed the door behind him. He caught the bag by the bottom corners and tipped the fish on the floor saying, 'Do you know where I found these?'

The doctor, having just suffered his second fright in less than twelve hours, did not reply, which was perhaps as well, for the patient went on, 'They were in the river, dead for the taking. It didna seem naitral, so I just brought them to see if maybe you could examine them with your microscope and tell me if they're all right. And don't say a word to a sowl.'

'You may be sure of that,' said the doctor. 'And if you'll just look in as if you were sick to the surgery in the evening I'll let you know.'

The shepherd, an obvious case of nervous exhaustion, was the first patient in at the six o'clock consulting hour and the doctor gave his report.

'I have examined these fish, John,' he said. 'And I'm sorry to say that I have found distinct traces of arsenic in them.'

'Och, that's too bad,' said the shepherd. 'I wonder, doctor, would you be good enough to get rid of the carcasses for me.'

'Gladly, John, gladly,' said the doctor, but it was the chelignite that he buried in a deep hole at the end of the garden.

31

CHAPTER FOUR

VILLAINS AND VOLUNTARIES

I WAS raised and nourished on the iniquity, the grasping worldliness and the vindictive chicanery of the Reverend Principal Robert Rainy of the Free Church College; a man in whose devious heart there glimmered not a spark of Christian brotherhood and charity.

This may sound a strange indoctrination to come out of a Free Church manse and from the lips of my Uncle George, who usually loved his fellow man even while rebuking him. To understand this amazing gracelessness — not in Uncle George, but in the object of his aversion — it is necessary to take a look at the painful circumstances of the birth of the Wee Frees; whom Principal Rainy would have strangled before they had the chance to draw breath.

It is a discreditable paradox that the Church of Scotland Free and Protesting was one of the first to abandon the stricter precepts of the Westminster Confession of Faith. Simply put, the Wee Frees are not the Church that their predecessors became in the generation following the Disruption of 1843; but are nevertheless the inheritors of the name and tenets of these founding fathers. And these are facts that were drummed into me long before I had a clue about the significance of what I was being told.

The trouble with the original Free Church, after its detachment from the Auld Kirk, was that as it swelled in numbers, in influence, in property and in funds, it steadily became more ecclesiastical than religious. And this is what sets Uncle George, not to mention my formidable grandmother, in their grand Calvinist context.

They both believed in Predestination and in man's natural depravity, and later had good cause to mourn man's inhumanity to man; the man, in their particular despite being the leader of their very own sect. I must plead guilty of a charge of partial counsel if I describe Principal Rainy as a trimmer, lax in doctrine and principle, a subverser of constitutions, and an opportunist 'skilled in the science of exigencies'; for I picked up these epithets when I was at my most impressionable.

In short Robert Rainy, the earliest of the rudimentary Scottish ecumenists, was the architect of the union of the old Free Church with the United Presbyterians to become the United Free Church. And to that end it was his purpose to disinherit the small protesting rump of Highland ministers and their flocks of everything that would lend them an identity — name, buildings and funds, and he nearly succeeded; which made him all the more peevish when at last, after three years of litigation, he failed in the House of Lords.

This is a story that is compounded of the classic malignance that luxuriates once pious folk fall out; it incorporates the Westminster Confession of Faith, the Longer and Shorter Catechisms, the Voluntary and Establishment principles, jolly hymns and minatory Psalms, kists of whistles, good old Calvinism and heretical Arminianism. All of these today are a *terra incognita* which might be none the worse of a word of profane exegesis.

The Church of Scotland Free and Protesting believed in the duty of the civil ruler to acknowledge and support the Church; and when the Disruption fathers separated themselves from the Church of Scotland in 1843, they did it saying:

'Though we quit the Establishment, we go out on the Establishment principle. We quit a vitiated Establishment, but would rejoice in returning to a pure one. We are advocates of a national recognition and a national support of religion and we are not Voluntaries.'

The Voluntaries were the successors of the Original Seceders, that equally quarrelsome congregation that spawned Burghers and Anti-Burghers, Auld Lichts and New Lichts and similar controversialists, most of whom were united only in their conviction that neither their spiritual independence nor their management of their temporal affairs were any business of the State. Of this company the

United Presbyterian Church was the largest surviving corporate institution.

But the United Presbyterians were also very strong on free-will and saving grace, subjects upon which the Westminster Confession was more than a little unyielding; and the Confession enshrined the uncomfortable doctrine to which the Free Church by its constitution was committed.

And that brings me back to Uncle George's bête noire, the unprincipled Principal Rainy who, revelling in the prosperity and influence of his denomination, hankered after the larger empire that he might command by uniting his 1068 congregations with the United Presbyterians' 593. But this accommodation presented problems, in the solution of which, though it took him some years, he demonstrated his genius for compromise and his implacability when contradicted by the fewest and weakest of his brethren.

First of all there was this awkward Westminster Confession, the strictures of which the United Presbyterians had already officially modified and softened. In 1892 the Free Church followed suit with a Declaratory Act designed to remove these established difficulties and scruples by denying Predestination, rejecting original sin, and disclaiming the more intolerant interpretations of the Confession. But adding a vague codicil to the effect that those who did not agree might personally stick to the old rule — provided they did it quietly.

This was too much of a concession for some, notably two aged Highland pastors, Donald Macfarlane of Raasay and Donald Macdonald of Shieldaig, who along with their elders and congregations separated themselves and formed a Free Presbyterian presbytery. They were joined by a considerable number of divinity students, among whom were Uncle George, John Macleod (who later became professor in the college of the purified Wee Free Church) and Alexander Stewart. And of course my widowed grandmother in Caithness. It was about that time that she withdrew from the vitiated church and started running her rival sacraments in the garden and back-yard across the road, which became a venue not short in eloquence and speaking to the Word, for she still had at her beck the itinerant 'Good Men' of the past; and them no longer inhibited by the formerly prior claims on the pulpit — in this case the tent — of the customary cohort of visiting assisting ministers.

Here I intrude a parenthesis to clear up a common — if not nowadays an important — misunderstanding. There may still be

some who vaguely remember hearing of what were called the Tent Missions; which evoked visions of devotions in a marquee. The 'tent' indeed was less pretentious, being designed only to keep the rain off the dissenting preacher on the hill or in the field. It was a wooden, sacking-covered frame, the shape and size of a Punch-and-Judy box, with a board for the Book, and a brass hook on the left-hand upright for the speaker to hang his watch on. Not that in those days much attention was paid to the passage of time, which tended to be measured more by the number of pan drops to be sucked than by the progress of the minute, or even the hour, hand.

But, back to the Free Presbyterians. Their reward for their loyalty to the faith of their fathers was to be stripped of any income, and turned out of their churches and manses. And with the encouragement of the representatives of the majority they were harassed by being excluded from such alternative places of Sabbath worship as the schools and public halls of their parishes. Yet they prospered and increased in their modest, if unbending way.

The next sticking point to a union with the Voluntaries (whose principles were less negotiable) was the question of the Establishment, which Principle Rainy allowed to go by default, an oversight that cost his party dear in the end. Robert Rainy was no committed Voluntary, but equally he was indifferent to the Establishment. He also, when it suited him, had an amiable regard for the Higher Criticism, even to the point of speaking up, at the first Assembly trial, in the defence of William Robertson Smith, the Free Church College professor of Hebrew at Aberdeen, who, after a second *fama* was expelled and dismissed the Church for saying in the *Encyclopaedia Britannica* that Moses did not write the book of Deuteronomy. In that verdict Rainy acquiesced.

The Free Presbyterians were, with characteristic charity and brotherhood, described as 'irresponsible weaklings, lacking even the ordinary elements of personality'. With these disinherited and safely out of the way, and with the Establishment principle nicely glossed, the way was clear — or so it seemed — to complete the exercise in ecclesiastical empire-building. A Uniting Act with the United Presbyterians was promoted and passed in the General Assembly of 1900. The new denomination would be the United Free Church of Scotland.

There were some two dozen dissenting ministers, mostly Highland, who pointed out that the majority had withdrawn from membership of the Free Church, and that it was therefore lawful for the minority to maintain the existence of that Church (as originally constituted); and for this purpose they would continue in session the following day and exercise all the powers of a General Assembly.

This, however, was not in the grand plan. The reply was an act declaring the United Frees to be the successor in office in all respects. This included the denial to the faithful rump of the right even to call themselves the Free Church. And plans for the future total terrestrial dispossession (as they had done with the Free Presbyterians) were initiated by having the doors of the Assembly Hall closed and guarded against the disinherited Highlanders.

All the trust property was appropriated. And although Uncle George never made much of the gesture, being always reluctant to grant grace to the Moderates, it was the Church of Scotland that came to the rescue of many of the north-country Wee Frees by sharing with them their places of worship.

The house of God now entered the temples of Mammon, and the victims appealed to Caesar, which was an unpleasant surprise to Robert Rainy, who had expected from them that meek forbearance which, his propagandists asserted, would have been only seemly. No other fraternal accommodation have been offered, the now nameless Wee Frees raised an action in the Court of Session claiming the whole Trust property. They did not expect to win, but they considered there might be some equity in a single test case. However with an eye to making the protest as expensive as possible the United Free lobby insisted that individual action should be taken against two thousand ministers — a ruse which finally recoiled upon themselves.

The first action in the Lower Court lasted five days, where the Free Church argued that the United Frees, having abandoned the Establishment principle were Voluntaries: that the new doctrine altered the prescribed attitude to the Westminster Confession of Faith: and that they, the dissenters, had an absolute right to refuse to enter the union.

They lost that case; they appealed to the Second Division, lost again, and the whole property was conferred on the United Free Church, leaving the minority, like the Macgregors of old, landless and nameless.

To the indignant surprise of the ecumenists the Highlanders, better advised than their opponents had ever expected, and with an equally unexpected and generous private financial backing, took the matter to the House of Lords, where the case was argued and the evidence was led over a period of two weeks. There were whispers that the decision might be in favour of the minority, but before it was ready for promulgation one of the Bench of Lords died; and a full re-hearing was ordered.

Up until that time, victory being certain, the Rainy camp had maintained a stiff-necked 'no compromise' stance. There came a conciliatory change between the two hearings in the Lords, when the verdict seemed less certain. The Wee Frees were approached with the suggestion that they should withdraw their appeal, and that a property arrangement might be come to.

But the dispossessed, being from experience properly suspicious, were no longer disposed to negotiate. The case went on, and the judgment, made in August 1904, declared that the United Free Church had no title, right, or interest in the property, money, lands or name of the Free Church of Scotland.

Then came the weeping and wailing and gnashing of teeth. The appellants were the true Free Church, and the inheritors not only of the tenets and faith of their fathers, but of great worldly possession scattered from the Pentland Firth to the Borders.

The consequent poor mouth on the part of the losers, the bleatings that a London-based House of Lords could not understand the subtleties of Scottish devotions, and other similar protestations of crying injustice (a changed tune) led to the appointment of a Royal Commission to assess these worldly goods, and to the passing of an Act of Parliament to redistribute them.

The Wee Frees certainly got their name back, but they did not do too well in the re-allocation in which Rainy tried to fob them off with a private settlement and an ex-gratia payment of £50,000. They lost their libraries, two of their colleges, and the Assembly Hall, a hard fact of which their fathers and brethren are reminded every year when they have to meet at their Assembly in a much inferior church hall just across the road.

These may come across as hard and unforgiving words, but I must plead that I learned them from Uncle George, who was always a most convincing teacher. And in later years, when I might have been tempted to mutter 'Now come on!' when he enlarged upon the polemical gifts, the opportunism, and the subversive genius of Robert Rainy, he was never slow to point out that during that nasty legalistic period he was himself your perfect objective observer, being neither a Free churchman nor a United Presbyterian, and certainly not a United Free; having been ordained into the Free Presbyterian Church at Stornoway when he qualified in the middle 90s.

With the House of Lords decision, he considered that the Free Church, purged of its sins and impurities, was now worthy of his presence; so he rejoined, proclaimed the word and prospered for five more years in Stornoway, and then for another thirty-four years at Fearn in the blander beinness of Easter Ross, where the farmers were wealthy, and might have patronised him, if Aunt Maggie had let them, which she didn't.

Granny, as I have suggested, was made of sterner stuff. She remained demonstratively Free Presbyterian; and was never blate to let her son-in-law feel his slight inferiority.

———— * ————

It is true that Uncle George's instruction of the young — at least this one — was selective. For example his unflattering feeling for the Moderates of the Auld Kirk left a few creditable facts which I had to look out for myself when, as it were, he wasn't looking. There was, for example that practical friendliness that its ministers showed during what might be described as Rainy's Highland Clearances.

Nor did he tell me that while the Free Church was among the first to modify the Westminster Confession as its prescribed standard for ordinations and teaching, it was the Church of Scotland that was the very last to desert it. Come to think of it, he could not have told me; for he had been dead for twenty years when, at the General Assembly of the Church of Scotland, the Moderator, Nevile Davidson, the Minister of Glasgow, said that the time had come for a new Assembly of Divines to rewrite the Westminster Confession, with particular reference to those terrifying questions in the Shorter and Longer Catechisms that deal with Election and Predestination. He pointed out that there was no declaratory act standing in the name of the Church of Scotland that authorised any departure from the letter of the Confession.

The Minister of Glasgow was not so strong, naturally enough, on the powers and duties of the civil magistrate. Though there is here an interesting revelation of the adaptability of the established Free Church in all matters of conscience and principle.

The Free Church of 1900 complacently abandoned Establishment to unite with the devoted Voluntary United Presbyterians. And during the following twenty-nine years so undermined their new partners that in 1929 the majority of these acquiesced in another union which brought the whole Voluntary boiling of them (former Seceders, Lichts, and anti-Burghers) back into the Establishment of the Church of Scotland.

It says a great deal, if not for the orthodoxy, at least for the persuasiveness of Principal Rainy and his disciples.

CHAPTER FIVE

UNCLE GEORGE LETS ME DOWN

I HAVE never lost my total belief in the influence that Uncle George was able to exert in the place where it most counted. This, by my reckoning was his own most Effectual Calling. And herein lies the only residual resentment I have about him. I came on leave from the RAF to be married in 1942, and he made the journey to Glasgow to tie the knot for us. But in giving us his blessing he suggested to the Almighty that for the future, in all my goings out and comings in, I should be provided with 'a modest competence'. I could wish that he had been a little more demanding; for he has been taken literally at his word.

The request did not seem unreasonable at the time, probably because my sense of values was somewhat distorted by the fact that my Service pay was two shillings a day.

———— * ————

There is another disappointment that I must record; but I do it with a fairly clear heart since it belongs to a generation that Uncle George just did not live to see. After some neglectful years I decided to visit the Free Church General Assembly at the top of the Mound in Edinburgh in the expectation of catching up on some of the salutary Calvinist doctrine and practice that I thought I had been missing.

And none of the Good Men of Caithness could have been any more sanctimonious than I was when, after one sederunt, I came out of the kirk door shaking my head and muttering: 'O, what a falling off was there.'

I was complaining on two counts. One, that just like it was across the road in the deliberations of the Auld Kirk, the eloquence was fiscal rather than saintly. I seemed to have stumbled in to the discussion on the report of something like the Sustentation Fund, or the Maintenance of the Ministry.

The other painful impression was that the habits of the non-conformist ministry had become excessively up-to-date — and conformist. The habits I speak of were not their foibles, but their vestments. Gone was the wideawake 'Shakespeare' collar and the white-tape tie. They were all wearing dog-collars. And in my day these were the headmark of those who did not mind if their flock played golf on the Sabbath.

They were not even wearing the detachable starched cuffs which I had so often seen go flying over the heads of the elders' enclosure when an overarm gesture proved to be too impetuous.

Incidentally the dog-collar as the uniform of the preacher is not nearly as old as one might think. Not only was it invented in the Church of Scotland, but I can tell you the name of the man who perpetrated it. He was the Rev. Dr Donald Macleod of the Presbytery of Glasgow, who became Moderator in 1894. During a debate on dress in the Presbytery in the year of his election, he intervened to make his claim, saying:

'The Church in the past had the great commonsense to leave the matter to the instincts of the ministers. Personally I have only one claim to immortality, and I am afraid it rests on a fact known only to myself and that is: I was the first to introduce what is known as the dog-collar in my youth 39 years ago. I did it. It is now recognised as the ecclesiastical collar. I hope that my claim to immortality on that account will be taken notice of by the historians.'

There is however one bit of Uncle George's clerical dress that survives. It is a small bit, real if unrecognisable as the only remains of his heavy black silken Moderator's gown. After years of hanging in a Highland wardrobe the moth and the rust got at it. But a fragment was saved and for the past twenty years I have worn it from time to time, on formal occasions. My mother, who like Granny was a good seamstress, took a six-inches-wide strip of the best part, and turned it into an evening dress cummerbund — an appropriately reversible one, for the other side, more flamboyant, is a gash of her own red Sinclair tartan.

—— * ——

When I left school in the late 20s I still maintained, if more sporadically, my contact with the manse at Fearn. But my terms of reference, both in matters ecclesiastical and moral were considerably widened when I took up the family trade of newspaper reporting; and went to Perth, where I found that ministers did not only wag their pows in pulpits, but turned a nearly honest penny as district correspondents, and contributors to the by-lined columns of weekly newspapers.

None of these, I should say, were Wee Frees, and I did not bother to mention them on my visits to Uncle George.

Nor, in fact, did I pay much attention to what they wrote. But I did enjoy, and have remembered their relaxed, anecdotal visits to the reporters' room when they had delivered their copy. Neither their gossip, nor their reminiscences were remotely pious — which was a change from what I had been accustomed to at the hands of the typical Free Church 'supply'; or at the feet of the formidable task force of mature divines who assembled as back-up to the Sacraments.

True, these newspaper exchanges had to do with the ministries of the raconteurs, but these touched rather upon the worldlier diversions of their parishioners.

For example, there was the Rev. David Graham of Redgorton, namely in his day as a pillar of the Church, an expositor of great weight, and a hebdomadal journalist of considerable philosophical respect. What improving recollections might I have of him! But, no. What remains is his telling us how, on holiday, he had found himself in a neighbouring parish church on a Sunday morning when the resident minister fell suddenly ill. He was button-holed, and asked to stand in. He had no sermon circulating in his mind; but, being an experienced professional, he knew that with the help of a couple of references, a text, and the accumulated phrases of past discourses, he could cobble a passable dissertation in half-an-hour.

To that end he allowed himself to be escorted to the vestry, where, turning to the beadle, he asked: 'Have you got a Concordance, that I might use for a minute?'

'I'm that sorry,' apologised the beadle, 'There isn't such a thing in the place; but if you look in that cupboard there, you'll find a wee po.'

A.W. Groundwater, another of our gossips, was the Congregational minister at Coupar Angus, and I remember him only as a demonstrator of tactful semantics. He had been approached by two local girls who were applying for a job in service at Glasgow and were asking him for a character reference. His problem, he explained, was (ministers being all-seeing) he was aware that these were frail sisters with a reputation for 'importuning men'.

'I could not tell a lie,' he said, 'but neither could I take the responsibility of perhaps spoiling their chances of a decent employment. So I wrote the reference, but said only: "To the best of my knowledge these are two very obliging young women."'

My natural affection for my uncle; my admiration of his militant steadfastness in the ever-present intrusion of original sin and man's depravity, has never mitigated my enjoyment of another Gaelic preacher and scholar, of whom he would never have approved.

The Rev. Dr Kenneth MacLeod of Gigha in the Established Presbytery of Kintyre, believed in fairies, and could make others believe in them too. He had two rowan trees at the churchyard gate to

keep the witches out. His church stood on a little eminence called Cnoc-a-Chiull, which means the hill of the music, and it was his pride that it was the only church in the Synod, if not indeed in the country, that was sensibly built on a fairy ring. Once on the eastern slope, where one of the buttresses joins the turf, he had me put my ear to the ground to see if I, too, could hear the music. He said it was there for them that had the grace to hear it. And, since he was a man whom I would not for the world have disappointed, I heard it.

He shared his manse with a ghost, young, pleasant and female. She made no noise and was not melancholy, but just drifted through the rooms pointing to the places where the absent-minded incumbent had mislaid things.

His closest and oldest familiar — none other than the elder Angus MacVicar — who like himself loved his fellow-presbyters but was impatient with presbyteries, once explained Kenneth to me as being one-third Presbyterian, one-third Papist, and one-third pagan. For myself I held him to be fully one-half pagan; and none the worse, but all the more felicitous for that. He was, as Angus MacVicar said, a mystic, a scholar and a sennachie, who preached with a light touch of tolerance and no brimstone; who could not utter a phrase that was common, any more than he could do a thing that was mean.

—— * ——

Although there was only one Wee Free, there has been quite a number of ministers in my family — though I must confess these belonged to my paternal, Aberdeenshire side. And they were all Moderates. Naturally enough there are no family legends about the quality of their preaching. Oral tradition always seems to be concentrated in the maternal line.

My grand-uncle (who used to write leading articles on education for the Glasgow Herald), was the Rev. Dr John Watt of Anderston Parish Church in Glasgow; while his brother Alexander, a person of much more modest ambitions and accomplishments, was the minister of Harthill in Lanarkshire. And then there was their cousin, J.B.A. Watt, an infinitely more pretentious parson, also originally out of Kintore. He married well in Edinburgh, and sought to compile an impressive family tree; with none-too-well authenticated connections, like a 17th-century 'tutor' of Craigievar, who died mysteriously, at the bottom of a well 'for State secrets'. He also raked up another couple of the tribe who were understood to have been slain

44

at 'the Battle of the Bridge of Dee'; an engagement, apparently, much neglected by the historians.

This cousin was the contemporary of John Watt who relied upon himself rather than upon his ancestors for whatever prestige he aspired to. They corresponded regularly. And, in the course of this communication, the other 'invented' an unmatriculated coat of arms, which he had engraved as a letter-head for his stationery. I cannot now recall what exactly the armigerous devices were; only that the motto on the subjoined scroll was 'Fides et Fiducia'.

On receiving the first of these noble letters, Grand-Uncle John, with all the traditional candour of a cousin replied; and at the top of his notepaper he added his reaction to the coat of arms. With his own hand he drew a cock crowing on a midden, with the motto 'By Cheek and Impudence'.

While I am upon the parallel family record I may add of this reverend cousin-once-or-twice-removed, that he kept his important in-laws, and indeed his own brood, well away from Kintore where his father, the local chemist, had been known to his fellow townsfolk as 'Drogie' Watt. By a curious gloss, a couple of generations later this by-name had been transmuted to 'Dr Watt'; an illusion that was allowed to survive until another unkind second cousin (my father) set the record straight, some time in the 1930s. There had been mention of a 'family estate' called Babylon; and a grandson, intending a sentimental pilgrimage to look at the domain, had to be disabused and told as kindly as possible that Babylon was a row of four derelict cottages, known locally, and for reasons that are probably better not pursued, as 'Bay-blon'.

One of my other grand-uncles, Joseph Watt, was the medical doctor at Turriff, whose junior assistant in the practice had once been the man who became Sir Arthur Keith, the anthropologist. But Uncle Joseph was dead long before my day, having, by all family account, been driven into an early grave by a harridan of a wife. He and his brothers (who included a grocer and a Clyde shipyard pattern-maker) were typical of another eident and self-reliant time in north-east Scotland, having come off a tiny croft, run by their widowed mother. The matriarchal influence was strong there, as it was in Caithness.

My paternal grandmother was one of their sisters. And fast to dispose of this lot before returning to the more sanctified fastnesses of Ross-shire and Caithness, the eponymous Phillipses were a sea-faring tribe (presumably originally out of Wales), my great-grandfather having been the commodore, under sail, of the Aberdeen trading smacks, which took salt herring to Russia, and brought back Archangel tar. He it was who took the first vessel out of Aberdeen Harbour under steam.

My grandfather, who was a schoolmaster, lost his taste for the sea as a very small boy. The deciding factor was that once, when he was taken on the voyage as supercargo, he fell overboard into the harbour at Archangel. The visible memento of that generation is a portrait of my great-grandmother, painted by her kinsman John Phillip R.A., who had a rare eye for a dramatically good-looking woman. He was a Victorian best-seller, still fairly well-known to art historians as 'Spanish Phillip' for his pictures of the Andalusian gypsy women and flamenco dancers of Seville.

There was also a great (or great-great) grand-uncle, who was the factor at Slains, and is memorable only for having (reputedly) run off to the West Indies with one of the daughters and heiresses of his employer, the High Constable of Scotland. This is a liaison which has always been recalled in somewhat hushed tones.

CHAPTER SIX

IN DANGEROUS COMPANY

B ODILY, as a small and amenable fat boy, I was considerably safer in the staid surroundings of the manse at Fearn than I was in the hands of my other uncles and cousins on the Caithness hills, where, in the idler moments of peat-cutting and sheep-shearing and dipping, they tended to become experimental and jocose.

I was never baptised by total immersion in the dipping fank, although it was mooted, and I maybe needed it; but I have had my hair cut. They did it, by sheer good fortune without drawing blood, with those fearful triangular bladed sharp shears. (Those were the days before electric clipping machines.) And that was the only time I have been barbered in the presence of a panel of inventive spectators suggesting refinements as the clipping went on. The definitive decision was made after the first few trial snips, when someone said: 'Ach, just gie him a dossan!'

The dossan was a common — and avowedly hygienic — hair style for country boys, with a single tuft left just above the brow, and the rest of the head clipped almost to the bone.

At the end — with my dossan not noticeably different from the scalp-lock that was left on the heads of the Mohican Indians to lift them up to the happy hunting ground — the operation was declared a hilarious success. That was until someone said: 'What will the weemen say when we get him back home?'

They said plenty.

—— * ——

The more elaborate 'high jeenks' (as Para Handy called them), in the execution of which no labour was considered to be too much trouble, found their fulfilment at Halloween.

There was the occasion, while the family slept, when the raiders, silently in the dead of night, dismantled the farm cart — five-foot-high wheels, axle, shafts, bed and sides — and carried it piece by piece through the low door into the kitchen, where they reassembled it. The last operation was to lead in the horse, harness him into the cart and tether him to the lamp-bracket above the fireplace. And steal away, leaving a substantial surprise for the family when they came down for their breakfast.

The retaliation the next year, more spectacular but less droll, was another silent night operation in which all the neighbourhood's movable farm machinery was collected and arranged like a Royal Highland Show display stand in the middle of the river. Also, Caithness peats, unlike those from other parts, are about a foot square and two inches thick, and just right for laying across the top of a nicely smoking chimney-pot.

—— * ——

Twice, at the end of the long summer holiday, I elected not to return to Glasgow and to the sub-urban sophistications of Bearsden and New Kirkpatrick Higher Grade School; but to remain in Easter Ross and spend the autumn and winter terms at the one-teacher Balmuchy School, just up the way at the cross-roads where the road to Tain began.

This, in its own right, was an extremely libéral education, where I learned much, including 'the worst word in the world'.

There were certain initial obstacles to overcome, which I flatter myself I accomplished fairly painlessly. Coming as I did from the manse, this had a good deal to do with the language of the playground. There were deeply ingrained illusions and reservations about such as myself, particularly among contemporaries who had been accustomed to hear of me from their parents as 'the meenister's boy'.

This lent me an odour of sanctity that was in need of dispelling, a task which I accomplished as quickly as possible by parading an

48

acquaintance, if not indeed a fluency, in a vocabulary of quite short words from my own unregenerate education in the godless South. Thus I established some underground empathy with the new company.

I had already learned some domestic discretion from the experience of repeating in the wrong setting the Gaelic pleasantries in which some of the young fishermen of Balintore had rehearsed me. So for the moment I stuck to the English, and having proved my reliability was, upon a bloodthirsty oath of secrecy, confided the worst word in the world by the son of the second cattleman at the adjacent farm of Balmuchy.

The peculiarity of this perfect monosyllabic shibboleth is that, so far as half a century of research and inquiry have been able to inform me, the word is known to be wicked only to me and to what survivors there may be of that little company of north-country subversives. I have cherished it because all these years it has given a splendidly esoteric quality to my own most depraved moments of profanity, or indeed obscenity. It has lent me a gratifying sense of lubricious superiority when I have heard others use it in innocence, for it is a very ordinary word.

It may seem an inexcusable breach of a long trust, but I am fain now to reveal that the word is 'burd', and am content, without any other hints, to leave it to the etymologists.

———— * ————

Conforming to the customs of the peer group presented other problems which precipitated me into other lies and deceptions. These made me passingly grateful that I did not belong to another (much deplored) communion, which would have required formal confession to the nearest cleric. And in my case I knew only too well who that would be. The other lads, in the summer and autumn, went barefoot. It was Aunt Maggie, who was strong on what was seemly, who laid down the law; and so I set out each morning decently shod in stockings and good stout polished boots.

Fortunately for my good standing, by the roadside just round the first bend from the manse there was a convenient hole in the dyke, which received the embarrassing footwear and kept it safe until I came home from school. Not that there was anything very singular about this evasion, as I learned only recently while reminiscing with my former editor of the Glasgow Herald, who also came out of a

manse (I make nothing of the fact that this was a 'Moderate' one, and that he was sent to a country school in Perthshire). He also planked his boots and socks by the roadside. And, even after all those years, we found common ground in recalling the characteristic delicate and mincing gait imposed upon us by the sharp, dry-stone metalling of the roads in the days before tar-macadam. It takes quite a time for soft, town-bred soles to become sufficiently calloused to take everything in their stride.

I had however one peculiarity of dress which was not so easily shucked, and I did suffer a little until the classmates got bored with 'Kiltie, kiltie cauld bum.' I did feel overdressed, though I did wear a jersey and not a jacket. It was, in fact a sort of secret comfort to know that the only pair of trews I had were so indecently holed that even Aunt Maggie had given up trying to mend them. I was also a little self-conscious about the kilt itself. It was not as masculine as I could have wished, being attached all round the top to a sort of black sateen liberty bodice. That however was a girlish secret that I kept more urgently than any concern about possible indecent exposure at the other end.

In his capacity as an ex-officio member of the County School Board and tester of Christian knowledge, Uncle George was an occasional visitor who gave me some misgivings to begin with. But to his credit he passed me by without a flicker of recognition. That may have been because — his questions being mainly about God and the Shorter

Catechism and such like—he already knew only too well how versed, or how ignorant, I was about such essentials. The satisfactory spin-off from the neglect was that he did not notice my bare feet. Or if he did, he never mentioned them either to myself or to Aunt Maggie.

As for the classroom and the three Rs, the most interesting, and noisy novelty, was the transition from jotters to the slates upon which we scratched out our lessons. Scratch was the word, particularly when one was lucky enough to find a defective slate pencil. I never went deeply into the technicality of this phenomenon; the end result was satisfactory enough. I imagine it had to do with the presence in the stub of pencil (theoretically softer than the slab of slate upon which it was supposed to write) containing an extra hard nodule of stone. Its effect was a high scream which set every tooth on edge throughout the whole inextensive building. And the beauty of it was that one could plead complete innocence, an absolution that was denied us in Bearsden when we sought to enliven the acoustics of the classroom with the deft vibration of rulers on the desk, or the humming noise that could be made to wax and wane across the room while the teacher looked in vain for its source.

Our slates at Balmuchy were chequered in red on one side. That was for sums. The other side was lined for pothooks and letters. There was a little sponge that we used for erasing our redundant exercises and additions and subtractions; but not always. And here I must come back to the demotic language which, under stress, sometimes intruded upon the more placid exchanges of instruction. On occasion there might be a permanent quality about the inscriptions on the school slate. A contretemps epitomised in the following authentic exchange, which discretion requires that I do not identify with Balmuchy School (though where else could I have heard it?) And, permissive society or not, I am too inhibited to spell it out, but anyone who has been either at school or in the Royal Air Force, will be perfectly able to fill in the blanks.

'Please Miss; Donny Munro has writ * * * * on my slate.'

'Then rub it out, Willie, just rub it out.'

'Please Miss, I cannae. He's writ it with a * * * * * * * nail.'

There were other extra mural skills that I learned from my sojourns at Balmuchy. I became adept in the country version of the marbles game of Moshie, the requirement for which was a sand playground in which it was not too difficult to dig hollows with our well-calloused bare heels.

But prime among the ploys and jolly wheezes was one unknown to the boys of Bearsden, my other confederates. There we had been obliged to introduce diversions into dull autumn evenings with such anti-social street games as 'clockworks' — to the annoyance of the residents of Collylynn Road — and ringing doorbells and running away.

In Ross-shire, on the other hand, I was introduced to a very instructive variety of animal management; which we practised with great hilarity, and some danger, in the byres of the large and prosperous farms with which we were surrounded. My instructors were the sons of these same farms. The idea was to wait until the byre had been mucked-out and sluiced down preparatory to the milking; when the cattlemen had gone home for their teas, and the milking women had not yet put in an appearance. During this pause, we sneaked into the shed, surveyed the long line of cows' rumps; and then, armed with a walking stick or the shaft of a hay-fork, went down the line tapping each cow smartly on a joint just above the root of the tail.

It took me a little practice to find always the exact spot, but on the whole this proved to be a satisfactorily splashy demonstration of practical animal physiology and natural functions.

I did not experiment much with the manse cow, since there, my own responsibilities being what they were, the exercise would have been self-defeating.

Though there was a full generation separating them, there was remarkably little difference between Balmuchy School, where I sojourned briefly just after the First World War, and the one-teacher-school across the road from the Caithness homestead, where my mother and her brothers and sisters learned their ABCs at the end of the last century. In the grey days of winter it was the paraffin oil lamps that leaked and stank. The single teacher, with a dedication that would be rare enough to find these days, juggled and organised his instruction among a score or more of bairns in ages ranging from five to ten or eleven. One practical responsibility, peculiar to Caithness, and the other Highlands, was that in winter each child carried, along with its satchel and its shining morning face, two peats from the domestic peat-stack, with which to keep the schoolfire burning.

However, in my mother's day there was no clock in the Westerdale school: not even a wag-at-the-wa'. No clock-watchers allowed. My grandfather, if consulted, would have said that the proper hours for schooling were from the rising of the sun to the setting of the same. He was no encourager of idleness. As for the dominie, he could always tell the time as accurately as he needed by the shadows on the floor and the way his pupils were wilting.

In those days faultless timekeeping was necessary only twice a year; on the occasion of the visits of the Inspectors, upon whose good report depended the continuation of 'The Grant'.

The scholars (the generic Scotch name for school bairns) never knew exactly what 'The Grant' was, except that it was something dreadfully important; and the only thing on God's earth, with the possible exception of a Liberal Parliamentary candidate, that could throw their master into an emotional panic.

This last might need a word of explanation; which is that the schoolmaster, one Johnston by name, if not the only Tory in a totally Liberal central Caithness, was certainly the only activist one — a status which he maintained by being bodily thrown out of every political meeting in the district between 1880 and 1920, including those held in his own schoolroom. He knew what to expect and faced these encounters well fortified in advance.

But back to the Grant; on the day of the visit not even the school-floor sundial was to be trusted. So a well-washed scholar with a good turn of speed was posted on the dyke a hundred yards from the school door to watch for the first appearance of the carriage and pair over Harpsdale Hill, a mile away.

The children were comprehensively scrubbed for the occasion, and so were their slates, which they had taken home with them the night before, so that they could scour the wooden frame with sand in the burn, and make it shine whiter than a properly-kept kitchen table. The whole ritual was too awful to be called in question, and it was only in later years that my mother and her siblings came to realise that, for all the warnings and coachings they had, they were seldom put to the question by the Inspectors. And the Grant went on. Indeed it was never in danger, although the schoolmaster's nerves never allowed him to be lulled into a sense of security.

The Westerdale school had the inestimable blessing of being the last but one on a long line leading from Thurso into the Caithness hills: and when the Inspectors descended from their carriage, it was the wise custom of the dominie to lead them straight into the schoolhouse, where he had prepared against their fatigue with a greybeard of the Real Ferintosh, and maybe a bannock. This made a favourable impression to start with. The mellowing, in fact, was so industriously applied that by the time they entered the classroom, it was usually sufficient for the children to look nice and bright. They contrived to do so, less from their sense of duty, than from the knowledge of what would be coming to them when the visitors had gone if they didn't.

It was also some contribution to those easy examinations that the Inspectors had already in their progress from Thurso visited seven or eight other one-teacher schools, in each of which the schoolmaster had made the same preparations for their refreshment.

—— * ——

I was led to believe, though I always knew this for propaganda, that Uncle George's early education at Swiney school, Lybster, on the coast, had been decorous and undisturbed; and one of the testimonies to his diligence is the silver medal (which I look at now) that he got from the Edinburgh Caithness Students' Association in 1887.

Aunt Maggie, I gather, picked up her Three Rs among some more boisterous rural distractions. My mother remembered an uninitiated pupil-teacher (from urban Aberdeen I think) who was sent to Westerdale once, while Dominie Johnston was recovering in bed from the combined after-effects of a more than usually physical General Election meeting.

This innocent had just started to call the roll when the badly snecked door burst open and a big, hairy, but friendly dog galumphed into the room. It did a zig-zag tour of the desks before skidding to a stop at the teacher's feet, where it laid down a lump of peat.

The class was unmoved, but a spokesman explained: "at's 'e ghillie's dowg. He wants ye to play wi'm.'

They watched, inscrutably, for a few minutes, while the pupil-teacher laboured to shift the dog, who was as heavy as he was playful. When the teacher was satisfactorily heated and defeated, my Uncle Dan, as expressionless as his classmates, rose from his place, and picked up the lump of peat. He walked to the door and pitched it into the playground, side-stepping smartly as the dog hurtled past him.

A few minutes later there was a great snuffling on the doorstep.

'That dog again?' says the teacher.

'No,' says Uncle Dan, who even then made a fetish of knowing everything, 'that Donald's dowg. He waits for him.'

And with that he went and opened the door to admit another full-speed collie, which having satisfied himself that Donald was present and apparently doing fine, retired quietly to the playground.

The next sound, with which the class was placidly familiar, was a series of high yelps, followed by a heavy thump and a burst of snarling. Here again Uncle Dan, ready with his running commentary, chipped in with, 'That's the schoolmaister's dowg. He's playing with Donald's dowg.'

This remained in memory because it was the only occasion my mother could recall when it appeared to be necessary to explain such an ordinary daily intrusion upon the opening routine of the day's lessons.

The dogs, in such a sheep-rearing territory, were as much a part of the community as the folk, and, having no doubt learned the habit at school when their masters were little boys, they came to church with the adults, and in my recollection were generally obedient and well-behaved. They did not as a rule get inside, though there were occasional cases of smuggling. They remained quietly in the churchyard, except in those special circumstances which went beyond the control of the sternest shepherd or the best-trained dog. The trigger was that strident soprano, who is to be found in every congregation.

There was such a soprano, more resonant even than Aunt Maggie,

who, at Westerdale, sat near the door. A dozen dogs or more would lie quietly among the gravestones until she led the praise. Then they would lay back their heads and sing too. There is no sound on earth like 'By Babel's streams we sat and wept' performed by a precentor, a gruff congregation, a strong soprano and a dozen collies.

My Uncle James was the flockmaster in the family, and he used to go out to quieten the dogs. But he had to shout very loud to pass through that sonic barrier, so that what he said to the dogs was often audible in the church. People going home from the service could from time to time be seen shaking their heads.

—— * ——

Uncle George never showed much interest in, or familiarity with those games of marbles notably the moshie variation of marbles, which he saw us playing in the sandy playground up the road from the manse. But I have often wondered whether it was as an observer or as an occasional player (as a young, and never joyless, minister in Stornoway) that he became so versed in the rules and techniques of the aggressive island game of Lotichan, or 'crofts'. I learned it and its Gaelic rituals many years later when as an aircraftsman in Lewis I was initiated into some of the diversions of the older schoolboys on the Eye Peninsula. On leave, and breaking my journey at Fearn to reminisce with an ageing Uncle George, I launched on a vivid description of this punitive game of knifie, only to discover that he knew all about it. An odd expertise, this, in a man of peace, for the essence of the competition was to mark long strips in the sward, one for each player, and, in turn from a standing position to throw a carving-knife (or ideally a bayonet) held by the tip of the blade, into the turf, then cutting out divots to the length of the penetration. They were all winners but one, and he the player who was last to excavate to the end of his row. His penalty was to stand with his back turned at the end of the court, while the others pelted him, each from his own pile of divots.

—— * ——

All schools have their sorrows, their misunderstandings and their injustices, and I had my share of these, in Ross-shire as elsewhere. So far as language was concerned I would have fared better if I had confined my expletives only to 'the worst word in the world'. The danger lies in being overheard, and it spans the generations.

There was one summer when, at some risk to life and limb with Uncle George driving the old and too-powerful Citroen, we motored from Fearn to visit the old home in Caithness, where Aunt Maggie's interest in the house, the way of life, and the inhabitants was undiminished to the point of lofty inquisitiveness. I have mentioned how more than once she got her answer from the tinkers. But she was ever undeterred. On this occasion the object of her benevolence was a small boy, Bennie, who came across the road from the school (still a one-teacher seat of learning) weeping bitterly— no, bawling his head off. She asked what was the matter: and he told her.

During the dinner-time interval, he had been lying face-down on the bank, gazing into the burn, and in his concentration he had not noticed the near approach of the teacher, who had forthwith taken him by the ear, led him back to the school, and given him a right good belting.

'Why in the world would she do that?' asked Aunt Maggie, 'What could you have been doing?'

'Ah was jist cursan the trooties,' sobbed Bennie.

Aunt Maggie let it go at that. But I took him aside later to ask what exactly he had been saying; but there was nothing new in it.

CHAPTER SEVEN

THE COURTSHIP OF UNCLE GEORGE

B EING, I presume, too young for such confidences —
even if they were otherwise freely communicable, which is unlikely —
I have never been privy to the details of Uncle George's courtship of
my Aunt Maggie. Except, that is, that, like the suitors of my other aunts
and my mother, he was subject to a rigidly timed discipline.

My grandmother, who was widowed in her middle-middle age,
when my grandfather was killed in a railway accident at Halkirk,
became the beloved autocrat of an extensive clan; and at the end of
her day, forty years on, she was still managing her far-flung family
from her bed.

I do not find it particularly easy to visualise Uncle George
wandering sentimentally hand in hand along the burn-side with Aunt
Maggie in the gloaming; but what I do know, I had from my mother,
who, no doubt in her time was subject to the same sanction.

Granny rose at daybreak, and she went to her bed at 9.30 in the
evening, taking with her the family Bible, and a heavy brass handbell.
Such authorised swains as were on the prowl were admitted (in
rotation) in the middle evening to the parlour, which was situated
immediately below Granny's bedroom. When she had composed
herself to her rest, having first 'searched the Scriptures' and read her
chapter for the night; and reflected upon the transactions of the day
and the tasks for the morrow; she would take up the bell from her
bedside table, and toll it. And she would continue the knell at five

minute intervals until she heard the click of the latch on the front door, and the fading footsteps of the amorous visitor.

My visual recollection of Granny is less peremptory. She was gentle and indulgent to her grandchildren, whom she addressed by the Gaelic endearment 'M'eudail', which means 'my star', and no one else has ever flattered me so; for nothing less stellar could be imagined than the solid round figure that I cut in those days — a circumference, truth to tell, which has not substantially altered in the succeeding years.

When we were expected, off the south train at Halkirk, Granny used to go out on to the grassy patch at the back of the house to watch for us. And when, for our part, sitting high in the trap as it breasted Harpsdale hill, our first sight of home, half-a-mile across the valley, was the black bombazine-clad figure, the raised hand of welcome, and the tricorned white lace widow's bonnet, with its black silk ribbon streamers floating in the breeze.

The cradle of my race was Westerdale in the heart of Caithness, a place which, with some exaggeration, my mother used to call 'the loveliest village of the plain'. It was certainly a place blessed with health and plenty; the health assured by Granny's simples, her sulphur-and-treacle in the spring, and her dreadful way with Epsom Salts. When we needed dosing, as when the first honey was taken from the hives, and we were allowed to wolf it at will straight off the comb, Granny mixed the medicine for us. A double spoonful of the salts melted in a half-pint of hot water. But her special method was not to administer the draught there and then, but to set the glass on the stone shelf of the milkhouse, to let it cool overnight, when it tasted infinitely worse — as bad, indeed as castor oil

Within a substantial circle around the homestead, which included the manse, the church, the grocery store, the mill, and a scattering of crofts and farms, Granny's distaff word was law, as the wives and sweethearts of the vicinity learned during the First World War, when, among other schemes for the comforting of the soldiers in Flanders, was one to provide them with good flannel shirts. I do not know what the central charitable organisation was, but it provided bolts of the cloth to groups of local women volunteers, for them to make the shirts.

At Westerdale the women met with their scissors and their needles and threads in the village schoolhouse, where they set about their labour. Or rather they had just got started, when my grandmother, then well into her seventies, stepped across the road just to see how they were getting on.

What she saw appalled her practical and economical mind. And with the authority which she arrogated quite naturally to herself, she ordered the women to stop what they were trying to do; to lay aside their scissors; and to fold up the bolts of flannel and to carry them across to the family house. There, Granny cut out the shirts herself, to her own long practised and expert pattern, and left her handless neighbours with the task only of sewing up the seams. I gather that not only did she get more shirts out of the material supplied, but that they fitted. Again I rely upon my mother's word; but apparently it requires a very particular skill to cut the neck-bands of mens' shirts so that they sit neat, with or without added collars.

My grandmother, Isabella, was a Mowat out of Strathnaver, whence her parents, crofters of Grimmore, had been evicted during the savage Sutherland clearances at the beginning of the nineteenth century. She was a kinswoman of the Reverend Donald Sage, the minister of the Parish of Kildonan, whose posthumous history, *Memorabilia Domestica,* is the standard, authoritative, first-hand account of the cruelties that were inflicted upon the peasantry by the creatures of the Duke of Sutherland; and particularly by the abominable Patrick Sellar, the land agent who was mainly responsible for turning the crofts of Sutherland into sheep-runs.

Like the others, my grandmaternal ancestors had their home burned over their heads; but unlike their less fortunate neighbours who were driven to emigrate or to try to scrape a meagre and unaccustomed living as fishers and shell-gatherers on the bleak and stony shores to the north of Helmsdale, they moved just over the border into the more humane estates of the Sinclairs of Ulbster, then represented by the great Sir John Sinclair, the agricultural improver, and the instigator of the *First Statistical Account of Scotland.*

Granny's parents found their refuge in the croft of Tormsdale on the Thurso river; just a step into the hill above Westerdale, where my grandfather would be establishing his own bein business as a cobbler and crofter.

That is another neighbourly courtship about which I know nothing. Suffice it that John Sinclair of Westerdale, boot-maker, wed Isabella Mowat of Tormsdale, and between them they raised our maternal clan.

I am not even sure where my grandfather learned his trade. His folk

were tacksmen farmers from the west side of the county, connected by name and descent as remotely as all tribal associations are, to the overlords of the territory, in this case the Sinclairs of Ulbster. Of these ancestors the earliest I know of is one John Sinclair who got into some bother by turning out as the second for William Innes, younger, of Sandside, in a fatal duel with Alexander Sinclair of Olrig. And the only other thing I know of him (he flourished circa 1711) is that he ate just once in three days — but enough then to keep a lesser man going for a week.

Anyway, Grandfather, the industrious young shoemaker, married Granny from up the river and brought her to Westerdale, where he had taken possession of a row of four or five but-and-bens, two of which he turned into his cobbler's workshop.

There were three or four cobblers in the workshop, with some chairs and seats on the window-sill for the constant but casual visitors who turned the place into a daily debating chamber. I can just remember some of the last of them sitting at their little oblong benches, stitching, fixing the inner welts with little squared wooden pegs, and talking, talking. My grandfather, himself, cut all the leather — as Granny did a generation later when she commandeered the bolts of flannel which her neighbours were failing to turn into proper shirts for soldiers. The standard products of the workshop were working boots of such a quality that emigrated customers from Caithness used to send them back from Canada for repair.

Granny, so austere in other matters, was extremely vain about the neat turn of her ankles and feet, a satisfaction which my grandfather enhanced by himself making her boots. These were not of ordinary leather but of black kid which he selected specially on his annual visit to the tanners in Edinburgh. These boots fitted like silk gloves, and Granny was so well provided that she was still wearing them to the end of her own day.

By all the hearsay that has come my way, my grandfather was what they called a 'great provider', and a fine business man to boot (in any way you look at that compliment). But he had his own innocence — and his pride. I am thinking about his gold watch. This was an American Waltham full hunter which he always wore. That is until the day he lingered too long on the fringes of the Thurso lamb-sales, where he was seduced by one of the fast-talking cheapjacks and 'won' (at what exact outlay he never admitted) a many jewelled, eight-day-guaranteed, Westminster-chiming, pure gold pocket watch.

When he brought it home his sons, more worldly wise than he, identified the case as pure brass, tried in vain to sound the Westminster chimes, and mocked him. He was much offended, and there and then swore that from then on this was the only watch that he would wear. The Waltham went into the sideboard drawer, and he was as good as his word; though they did say that within a few weeks when he was asked the time of day, he no longer reached into his vest pocket, but took a look at the sky to see in what airt the sun was riding.

In the rest of the house he and Granny started to raise their family of six sons and four daughters. He prospered, and brought down two living-in masons from Thurso, and between them they turned the two end but-and-bens into a two-storey family dwelling. The intervening but-and-ben remained, and it resides in the liveliest part of my recollection, because this was the family kitchen in which everything of immediate importance happened.

With the central partition taken out it was twenty feet long with an open peat fire at either end. And let me start with these. Each was a two-foot deep alcove, four feet across in the end wall. In the floor in the middle was a pit to receive the peat ash — the finest of powder which with its characteristic and nostalgic smell permeated not only the house but the very countryside: a welcoming reek that remains in the memory after half a century and more of coal fires and central heating. Across this little pit there were half-a-dozen two-inch strips of iron upon which the fire was built.

Above this, swivelled and anchored to the side wall of the alcove was the swee, with its arm stretched over the fire, and its adjustable hook for hanging the cooking utensils. And of these, two are un-

forgettable in their own right, the girdle and the pot-and-the-bools. The pot was the massive iron vessel capable of taking the haunch of a sheep or the better part of a side of bacon. It sometimes had three short legs, but it always had two lugs at the rim, to receive the bools. And the bools were a hinged, semi-circular hoop of round iron, with hooks at either end. Hung on the swee, this arrangement kept the pot nicely over the stacked peat fire.

The kitchen was the epitome of the self sufficiency of the way of life. Hung from the open rafters were the hams from the regular pig-killing. A messy and specialised business this, performed in the adjacent paddock by an itinerant expert, who straddled his upturned victim upon a sort of oversized saw-horse.

Along the back wall were the three massive wooden kists, scrubbed white, with their hinged lids for working surfaces, containing the seasons' supply of flour, barleymeal and oatmeal, packed and tamped down for their preservation so tight that when needed (and that was every morning) the grains had to be chiselled out with a heavy carving knife. The other essential, which stood just inside the back door, was the barrel of salt herring.

In my day, or indeed in my mother's girlhood (she being the second youngest of the family) there was plenty of help, and Granny did no domestic chores. That is but one. When her good china was used she had a basin of hot water brought to her from the kitchen, and she washed the cups and saucers herself, drying them upon cloths kept in a sideboard drawer, which none might use but herself.

For the rest she supervised; and there were established routines.

For example, every morning when the men had left to whatever their tasks were, in the byre or the fields or on the hill, the available women folk (of whom there never seemed to be any great lack) got yoked to the daily baking. They made white scones, treacle scones, barley scones, and oatmeal bannocks. 'Loaf-bread' as they called it, was an occasional and despised indulgence — this was a morning habit that Aunt Maggie took with her to the manse at Fearn. I ate the scone; but I best remember the sight and the bouquet of the oatcakes. They were rolled circular, to the diameter of the sixteeen-inch girdle, and they were at least a quarter-of-an-inch thick. When they were cooked they were set like barrel-lids round the sides of the fire alcove to crisp and curl in the wafted aroma of the peat smoke. And they remained to hand in that shape, on the dresser or on the table, when you helped yourself by breaking off what you wanted, and clarted it with butter and crowdie, adding, if your sweet tooth was tickling, a spoonful of rhubarb jam to the top of the crowdie. Rhubarb jam, incidentally, was the only home-made preserve that I remember clearly; I have the impression that it was bottled in quantity mainly to go with our rice-pudding.

There was no running water in the house, a lack which was accepted without complaint. The drinking and cooking water came from a spring on the other side of the road, and the washing water from a great tank of Caithness flags built on the outside of the back wall to catch the rain, of which there was usually an abundance.

Round the corner of the garden, against the southern aspect of the house, and embowered in honeysuckle, there was the earth closet, a remarkably wholesome retreat, though not specifically built for comfort. It enshrined the simplest, one might say the most fundamental, pleasures of a balmy summer's day. With the door open there was the calming and salubrious vista over the hedge of fuchsia and foxglove away to the blue distance of the mountain Morven, the only sizeable eminence in Caithness. The door opened inwards, which was clever, for at the sound of approaching footsteps along the pavement to the garden gate, it was but the movement of an instant to reach out your foot and kick it shut.

They counted themselves neither particularly hardy nor deprived. But we have seen changed days, even in Caithness, for now, with their store cupboards depending on the grocer's van with its convenience food, and even the winter feed for the stock held at a hopeful minimum, when the first bluffart of a snow blizzard comes sweeping across the Ord, we have the crofters on the hill bleating for the RAF helicopter and the emergency supply-drop.

My mother used to say that her brothers and sisters did not rate it a proper winter if they did not have to be dug out of the house at least three times. The house faced north-east, and had this peculiarity that both its doors and all its windows were on that side. And that was the direction the wind and the snow came from, so that it took only a moderate storm to have the drift high and right above the sash of the upstairs windows.

There was no fear of hunger, nor of cold with the peatstack at the door; and their other test for January was whether they could skate the Thurso river from Westerdale to the sea, a distance of some twelve miles.

For all our diesel and electric trains and our helicopters and snowploughs the older transport was better adapted for the storm. For long after the motor car had arrived, the first machine to break out of the snow-bound wilderness was always the old-fashioned farm cart with its pair of five-foot high ironshod wheels.

Indeed these wheels, and the five-barred iron gate to the school, recall one of the other diversions of the frosty winter, a somewhat masochistic one, for I am told that the children of my mother's generation could not resist gauging the intensity of the frost by sticking out their tongue and laying it against either the metal rim of a cart wheel, or the top rail of the school gate. If the tongue stuck, which it always did, then the weather was adjudged up to standard, and the teacher was summoned with a drop of hot water, or a glowing peat, to try to detach the tongue without flaying a whole layer of its skin.

—— * ——

The work ethic had always been strong in Aunt Maggie — stronger than in any of her siblings — and it was transferable.

She was some ten years older than my mother, and she took her turn at the household management with my other aunts, Jeannie and Helen who, along with Uncle John and Uncle Alec, comprised the senior end of the family. When Aunt Maggie was on duty the younger ones always sought to make themselves scarce, before being dragooned into water-or-peat carrying, dishwashing, sweeping and bedmaking.

When the junior half of the family outgrew the resources of the Westerdale school, they were sent to Thurso Academy, which took them away from home for the week. To meet this situation my grandfather took a place in Thurso, where, in turn, the older sisters acted as housekeeper and general manager. The favourite among these was Aunt Jeannie — who eventually had three husbands, and raised a tribe of her own in Canada.

She made no demands on her wee brothers and sister, not even asking them if they had done their homework. It was Aunt Maggie's horror of idle hands that got them down.

They came home for the week-end, and there was a routine about returning to school on Monday. The purpose was to try to miss the train at Halkirk Station; a hopeless ambition, for the one-legged stationmaster used to watch them dawdling over the last hill. And not only did he stand in the middle of the road, whistling and waving them on, but he held the train until he had counted them all on board.

—— * ——

My grandfather, who had an abiding sense of responsibility to God, had also an instinct for hospitality, as well as being a great provider. On the Wednesday before the Fast Day that talent found its highest expression, when he yoked the pony in the early morning and trotted off to Thurso, twelve miles away. About dusk he would appear again over Harpsdale hill, the pony would be walking, and the gig laden with beef and butter and white bread and a great many other odds and ends which my mother did not remember in detail. What she did remember, however, was the brown gallon jar of whisky, without which Communion at Grandfather's was unimaginable. The old Free Church had no inhibitions about the spirits; and it had a very hard head.

The provision was necessary, for on the five days of the Sacrament there would never be fewer than twenty at a meal in the house. And often dinner (pronounced denner) ran into two or three sittings. The platform from the school across the way would be brought in and set up on trestles in the living-room for a dining-table, and it would stay loaded until the last of the Good Men had tramped out of sight on the Monday.

The Good Men were the mainstay of the Caithness Communion. They were all characters, they all seemed aged, and they could pray. Throughout the summer months they trudged from Communion to Communion, speaking to the Word, and putting their blessing on those that gave them shelter. They travelled great distances on foot, with now and again a lift on some passing cart, and bore some resemblance to Elijah, who was so fortunate in his ravens.

In the evening they would begin to arrive, footsore and dusty. There were plaids on their shoulders. They would duck in at the low kitchen door, and a place was waiting for them by the fire. There was only time for the hat to come off and the staff to be laid along the top of the peat neuk before they were seated with a big glass of whisky in their hand.

Meanwhile some of the children, well experienced in the rite, had brought the basin of warm water and taken off the boots, and were washing the feet. I have always thought that was a very nice gesture, with something biblical in it. It certainly must have felt like welcome to one who had walked on a stony, unmade road.

Before it was time for the Books the important guests would all be there. Angus Morrison was a huge man, and blind. He came from Lewis, and always walked all the way, taking in the Communions up Strathnaver and along the Bettyhill side. As a young man he had worked in Canada and his languages were Gaelic and French. William Elder and William Murray were another two, notable only for their devoutness, but Adam Mackay had the memorable habit whenever he stepped over the threshold of booming in a great and solemn voice, 'Peace be on the house.'

Then there was John with the Big Head. My mother and my uncles and aunts never knew of his having any other name. His is, or used to be, a fairly common deformity, and he walked very slowly, for he had to balance the great head. His friend and companion on the road and his rival in the length of his prayers was Walter. Again there is no surname, but Walter was lame, and when he fell he could not rise till he was lifted. And the memory of Walter is that he was always either crying or laughing. Sometimes it was hard to say which he was doing.

These were the pilgrims who came to assist, and they were respected as a generation of godly men, who were never allowed to go hungry; who accepted hospitality and raiment with dignity and repaid it with their blessing.

With these men I must include my Great Aunt Bess, my grandfather's only sister. She was married to a farmer in the north end of the county and always came. I never saw her, but my mother's description is enough. 'Aunt Bess,' she said once, 'was a most unusual woman. She could stand up and pray like a man. And she brought up the wildest family that ever lived. I think it was only Aunt Bess's prayers that kept them from being consumed altogether.'

The Good Men, they had their failings too, and I have no doubt that in their moments of solitude they sought forgiveness for the impatience they sometimes felt at one another's habit of monopolising the Lord's ear. At my grandfather's table, even when it was twelve or fifteen feet square, there was a top place reserved for the elect. But it was frequently difficult when the elect were there in strength. Some of them have even been known to slip out of the service before the benediction in order to be first in that place — which carried with it the privilege of asking the blessing.

In later years, long after my grandfather's death, when the ceremony was still continued, but diminished by the passing of that generation, my grandmother once laboured under an almost comical anger when she came in from church to find that the place had been usurped by one whom she regarded as unworthy.

The Books came before bed, and the assembled family, seated through two rooms with the door open between, would pass the pile of Bibles and Psalm books round. They would sing a verse, read a chapter, and then one of the Men would pray. On ordinary days my grandfather did that, with reverence and reasonable brevity. But the Men did not bother much about time. I have heard by mother say that above them all Walter was a terrible fiend for praying. When at last he finished and the family rose from their knees the floor was always studded by half a dozen who had found a comfortable kneeling position and a soft chair seat for their brow, and had slept.

Then they were off to bed, but by five in the morning the more devout were up again and out at the dykesides praying on their own.

The children, of whom there were many, never considered it a proper Communion if they were able to sleep in their own beds. There were shakedowns all over the house, and the older boys were bedded out with neighbours.

Thursday was Fast Day and the services were long, but not nearly so long as on Friday, which was the Men's Day. It was then that those who felt so inclined spoke to the Word, and the congregation was lucky if it got home to its dinner by half-past four. It was all in Gaelic and they were very fluent.

At any time in those days the Fifth Commandment was respected to the letter. At Communion time it made Saturday night a fever of domestic scurry. Boots were cleaned, faces were shaved, the broth went on, and most of the other food was cooked. And a day's supply of peats was brought in and stacked near the fires. Not a dish was washed on Sunday. So on the last day of the feast the women folk did not see, or have time to care very much about, the departing guests.

Sunday was notable principally for the dreadful Presbyterian rite of 'Fencing the Tables'. In a milder form it is still practised. But in those days the minister came down from the pulpit, like the Avenging Angel, and aided by the assisting ministers, walked up and down beside the prepared tables calling on the congregation to take the Sacrament, but daring them to come on the pains of damnation if there was anything on their conscience. On these occasions even my grandmother could find herself in doubt; and it always took a bold one, and not always the holiest or most blameless, to be first to dare that accusing eye and come forward. Then the others trickled on.

With the new week the Good Men were off again, walking into the hills to the next Communion, and stopping when the spirit moved them, as it did with great regularity, to kneel by the roadside and pray. The sight of a venerable head bowed in the ditch was too common for ordinary wayfarers in Caithness to give any special notice.

They tell of one hot summer day when Walter and John with the Big Head were making their way from Strathy to Westerdale. It was a long and dusty walk and every now and again the fear of the Lord would come on them, and they would be down on their knees to put up a word. The going was slow, for John had to carry his head, and Walter was lame and had to be careful about not falling.

They were both kneeling when a farm cart trundled up. And John, who was practical as well as holy, and knew the distance there was still to go, said a quick 'Amen' and rose. He accepted the lift; but Walter gave no heed to the shake on his shoulder. He prayed on, and the cart, with John up, disappeared over the hill.

Half an hour later, Water closed his prayer and rose to his feet just at the moment when a carriage and pair bowled up. There was a liveried coachman driving and one of the visiting gentry in the back. Walter was hoisted aboard and was carried along at such a spanking trot that they soon overtook the farm cart and John.

As the handsome turn-out swept past, Walter, who, as you may understand, had a fine quoting knowledge of the Book, leant out, and waving his staff cried (in Gaelic, which sounds better), 'The chariots of the Lord twenty thousand are.'

———— * ————

The Good Men of the North who used to honour my grandfather's home at Communion time, held overflow services from the fast day to the Sabbath in a field at the back of the house and on a tulloch down by the river. For the rest of the year the 'tent' was kept in an outhouse along with setting hens and some odds and ends of farm machinery.

Though some of them may have been guilty of a little backsliding in later years, my mother and my aunts and uncles were trained in a healthy respect for an Almighty who worked his will in a good Scots manner with thunderbolts and a strong line in threats of hell fire and the wrath to come. What with family worship twice a day, including the singing of the Psalms (starting with 'That man hath perfect blessedness', and working steadily through them to 'Praise ye the Lord', and then starting all over again), my mother knew her Bible pretty well.

But the Shorter Catechism always got her down. Even after fifty years a haunted look chased across her face when she spoke of the Sabbath evening catechism. My grandfather, who in all other respects left the memory of a good and generous man, and not at all stern, on the Sabbath seemed to become invested with an awful omniscience. He knew all the questions and answers by heart, and he asked them in order round the family circle, including my grandmother (who was word perfect), the servant lassie (who was usually too afraid to speak), and the workmen (who were called in for the occasion and who 'gagged' glibly). These last were experienced, and, seeing the 'What is Sanctification?' coming when it was still half-a-dozen questions off, were sometimes able to dodge. The scene was etched deeply in my mother's memory. She often spoke of it, and I, who do not now know my Shorter Catechism as I should, was always charmed to listen, for I knew the room and the peaty smell, though the faces of those who were in it are not clear.

One summer we went to Gigha for a holiday. The Post Office at Gigha is also the general store, and when we walked in there one morning for a postcard and twenty cigarettes the postmistress was unpacking a crate of books. The school was opening the next day.

I was not paying much attention, but I noticed a nostalgic look in my mother's eye and followed the glance. She was staring at a pile of yellow-covered Shorter Catechisms. She picked one up absently, and without opening it said, more to herself than anyone else.

'What is Effectual Calling?'

And there was all the fellow-feeling in the world in the postmistress's voice as it came back, equally reminiscent.

'Yes. That was always the difficult one, wasn't it?'

—— * ——

My Cousin Mary, though she lived fifty years in Glasgow and died there, had her roots too deep in the peat banks of Caithness.

I call her my Cousin Mary; actually she was a sort of grand second cousin, being the first cousin and great crony of my grandmother.

I remember her as a very hearty old lady in stiff, black silk, with a round silver brooch. She is dead a good many years now, and only the brooch remains clear in my mind, because it looked so very like the florins she used to shed among us. The principal link in memory between her and Granny is that they both used to call me and the other children 'M'eudail', a Gaelic endearment, which always sounded strange and caressing and so superior to the common and understood pet names that the neighbours' bairns had to make do with.

I cherish her memory, too, because she is a personal link for me with the trial of Madeleine Smith. She comes late, it is true, into that story, but as a young lassie new out of Caithness she was nurse in the household of William Minnoch, çi-devant betrothed of Madeleine. Unfortunately during Cousin Mary's lifetime I had not yet become interested in the cause-célèbre, and so did not know to ask her if the dread name was ever mentioned. I console myself that it is unlikely. By that time William Minnoch was married and the father of a family, and they were still living in an age when, even discounting a natural personal wish to forget it, the adventure of Emile l'Angelier and Madeleine Smith would not be regarded as suitable instruction for the young or for their nurse.

—— * ——

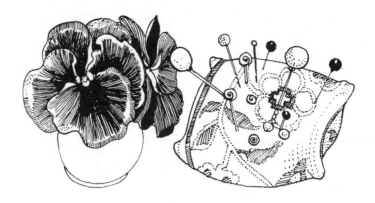

Every other year Granny used to pay a state visit to Glasgow from Caithness. She came primed with gossip and reminiscence, with reports of them that were dead and stories of them that were still alive. It was a great and contented time for her and Cousin Mary and for another friend and cousin, a Mrs Bain, who was of an age and had the same background of sib gossip.

The day after she arrived, about one o'clock, a cab would call for Granny, and off she would go in a dignified flutter, her silver spectacle case swinging from its silver chain at her waist and a neat little black basket in her hand. The basket contained the well-starched widow's bonnet that she always wore indoors.

The cab would collect Mrs Bain on the way, and then on to Cousin Mary's, where they would spend a glorious afternoon, the three of them sitting round the fire in the drawing-room drinking a ceremonial tea, and, I believe, a little something to keep out the cold. And they talked themselves tired, for no one dared to interrupt or intrude upon the cherished rite.

About seven at night the cab would return Granny to us replete. These cracks were life itself to the old ladies; they knew each other so well and had few secrets.

Before Granny went back north the same formality had been gone through another twice, in Mrs Bain's house and ours. And yet there was always an intangible restraint, a feeling of something unsaid. But it was none of our business, and there was not one of us who would have dared to mention it.

—— * ——

Many years ago, when they were still pioneering the West in covered waggons, Cousin Mary saw her girlhood sweetheart off to Canada. He was going to make good (and he did), and she was going to follow him. She was a handsome and capable girl, so she wiped away the tear and spent the next year in the employment of the Minnochs gathering a sensible pioneering trousseau. When the word of bidding came she was off for Canada on the next boat, with a lot of useful things in her trunk, and even a fine respectable broadcloth wedding suit for her 'intended'.

Cousin Mary had an attractive way with her, and she was strong willed, and on the ship she met Robert. Robert was nearly middle-aged, and had been on a trip home to put a stone on his wife's grave. He was returning to his farm in Ontario.

I said that Cousin Mary had a native charm, and when the boat docked she and Robert were married at once.

The relatives at home, and her former employers, who had grown very fond of her, were startled and raised a great fuss, for Canada was a long way off and Mary was young and Robert was unknown to them. So her brother was sent to bring the couple back to Scotland, where Robert was set up in the scrap iron business by the Minnochs, and did very well at it.

At decent intervals Cousin Mary had by him a small and expensively educated family of well-to-do and socially industrious sons and daughters. Mary herself died, in the fulness of her age, still with a Caithness accent and a compromising sense of humour.

—— * ——

For many years these meetings I have spoken of went on. Then one day — I think it would be about the year 1926 — Granny came home with a weary but settled and satisfied look about her. Her hands twittered a little as she undid her bonnet strings and she said — 'She sent it to him.'

We were mystified, and Granny went on to explain in an awed sort of voice that they had been sitting at tea when she suddenly found herself saying, 'Mary, whatever did you do with that suit?'

And Mary had explained without any hesitation or surprise at the question.

'I posted it to him from Montreal.'

It took fifty years to ask that question, but the final content that came with the resolution of that gnawing curiosity was well worth the wait.

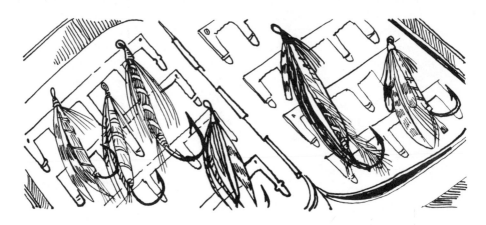

CHAPTER EIGHT

A PERMISSIVE INTERLUDE

In my early teenage a certain restlessness intruded upon the tranquil and regulated piety of the long summer holiday in the Free Church manse at Fearn. I was reacting to the siren calls from five or six miles to the north — from Tain on the Dornoch Firth. There my Uncle Dan, long-widowed, and the most heretical of Aunt Maggie's younger brothers, with a family of six, was the North of Scotland Bank agent.

Theirs was a more relaxed and permissive lifestyle, and it was with some reluctance that I was released to join them in an extended visit. The reluctance had to do with Uncle Dan's freedom of expression, a moral peril of which I was made aware by overhearing Aunt Maggie saying, 'And you know, he swears in front of the children.'

With my long prior knowledge of the worst word in the world, the warning, to say the least of it, made the projected visit all the more promising.

Nor was I disappointed when soon after I had been deposited in the bank-house in Tower Gardens, he breezed in for his lunch, reporting as he threw his hat at the hall-stand that he had just seen one of their more perjink neighbours weaving his way down the High Street.... 'And he's as happy as a thoosand buggers,' thus setting a tone which proved to be entirely satisfactory. I did not go to church for more than a fortnight; and Sabbath evening worship was replaced by a more harmonious, but secular praise in which Uncle Dan scraped his fiddle, my cousin Isobel (who was an LRAM) thrashed the piano, and the rest of us gave voice to a catholic repertoire which ran from 'Ae fond Kiss' to a contemporary ballad that had as its first two lines (if they were not, indeed, the title of the piece), 'If you Want to Keep Your Wife at Home, Never Let her Learn to Dance.'

The other diversions were equally unaccustomed, but instructive, being substantially unsupervised. My cousins for example introduced me to the financial satisfactions of caddying on Tain's championship golf-course. This patently was a fringe benefit that cast no shadow on the social prestige, such as it was, of the senior banker in the town. Uncle Dan, indeed, encouraged such self-help. Even in the company of his more important bank customers it caused him no embarrassment, but rather induced him to step aside and ask us loudly how our prospects for engagement were going, when he found myself and another couple of members of his own brood touting for trade on the open space outside the professional's shop door. Mine, however, was a brief prosperity, for the wife of one of Uncle George's wealthier parishioners not only recognised me, but nearly employed me, and went straight back and reported the encounter to Aunt Maggie, who had me back at the manse within 24 hours. There I was roundly lectured upon the dignities and obligations of my position as 'the minister's boy'. Uncle Dan had interceded a little, but to no avail. He was one of Aunt Maggie's younger brothers, and accustomed to losing arguments with her. As for myself I did try suggesting that for years I had never been discouraged from the parasitic habit of receiving unearned tips (even half-crowns) from departing guests from the manse, and that surely it was more honourable to be rewarded, quite modestly, for the honest though modest task of humphing somebody's bag of clubs round a golf course.

But all the answer I got was: 'Your Uncle Dan should know better. But he never had any proper idea of the duties of his position . . . or ours.'

That may have been true enough, but he was successful in his own calling, and was in fact the ground landlord of the fishing village of Hilton of Cadboll which housed the most devout members of Uncle George's congregation. And it disturbed Aunt

Maggie that, him being her brother, he did not qualify as a good example.

But Uncle Dan was easy to get on with. His was the only bank manager's private office in my experience where clients, importuners, or just cronies in for a crack, were received in an atmosphere blue with the reek of Bogey Roll, which he smoked in an eroded blackened pipe to the amount of an ounce a day. The pipe was fitted with one of those old perforated metal caps over the bowl to keep the sparks in. Incidentally, this was a most useful piece of equipment because in emergencies he could shove his still-lit pipe into his pocket without any serious danger of setting his jacket on fire — an accident to which Uncle George was prone.

The furnishing of Uncle Dan's office desk was also pretty basic. In fact I thought it rather old-fashioned until I realised that the jar at his left hand was not filled with quill pens, but with the supply of hens' feathers that he kept for scouring the stem of his pipe. Like all twist addicts, he was a wet smoker. I never noticed what he did about that; but there was a fire-place in his office.

Among his male in-laws, and essentially on matters of the spirit and Sabbath observance, there was a tacit understanding to avoid confrontation with Uncle George — a discretion in which he acquiesced. What was not taken into calculation until it was too late, was the rebellious influence which Uncle Dan could have upon the young. And I was the innocent who sparked that one off.

It occurred during a rare coming together when there was a mass holiday descent upon the homestead in Caithness. In the inciting presence of my cousins, and over some trivial prohibition,

I had a tiff with Uncle George, and was publicly rude to him, using some such inexcusable phrase as 'What the Devil?'

The breach was total, and since there was just a little bit of right on my side, Uncle Dan (who now spoke my language) took my part and urged me to hold on, with such justifications as 'You're quite right,' and 'Who does he think he is?'

But it was my Uncle Alec, older, and the family peace-maker, who took me aside, without an audience, and told me: 'Go on boy. Go and tell him you're sorry. You've nothing to lose.'

While I have the warmest, and earthiest, recollections of my Uncle Dan, his late wife Martha, whom I can hardly remember, had not been *persona grata* with my immediate family — at least with my mother. This was because at her first sight of my young brother, who as a mewling infant was shown to her, her only comment (much quoted in after-years) was: 'My, my. But isn't he affa wee?'

—— * ——

The homing instinct was highly developed in our branch of the Sinclairs, and the first of these to react to it was Uncle Dan who, when he retired from the Bank, bought the old Church of Scotland manse in the township of Halkirk. As I knew and enjoyed it, it was a rambling, comfortable and hospitable house, made for male chauvinist occupation; with no cretonne, but full of chairs made for yarning in, and moulded to the backsides of those that habitually used them. There was something subtly welcoming about the ring-marks of the bottoms of glasses engraved into the leather arms of the easy-chairs.

The entrance hall and the drawing room were more like an

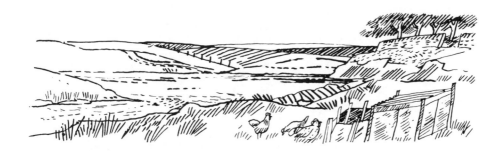

armoury, with their cabinets of shot-guns and fishing rods, and there he entertained to his taste, and to my edification, such cronies as John Abrach Mackay, the greatest of Caithness anecdotalists and north-country propagandists.

It was not a particularly quiet house, any more than the Tain demesne had been, for his was a family that conducted its discussions and little disagreements at full voice. But you always knew where you stood, if you could shout loud enough. The amenities included the Thurso River, which flowed past the bottom of the garden, and included, so handily, some tempting pools. It was, indeed, on the stretch below the house that the Queen Mother, during her summer holidays at the Castle of Mey, sometimes came to fish for salmon. On these occasions she had informal, and rewarding contacts with some of the village folk, whose expertise on the river had not been all that legitimately acquired.

It was one of these worthies who, on being cross-examined on his meeting with her, could move himself to reply, with total enchantment, only: 'She shook hands wi' me. She's got a wee, saft handie on her — like a bairnie's erse.'

It was, no doubt, relief to Uncle George, let alone Aunt Maggie, that it was an old 'Moderate' manse that Uncle Dan had converted to his unhallowed use. It was certainly there that we, the cousins, armed ourselves when we set out on our little private expeditions into the hill and up the further reaches of the river.

—— * ——

78

Then there were my mother and my older brother, a general practitioner (a title that might be extended a little to include some of the inborn free-fishing instincts of the family); who, soon after the War settled in Dunbeath, only a moderately long stone's throw from Uncle George's native Lybster.

I myself came back there every year to recharge my editorial batteries with the folk-lore and clash of one of the more stimulating and disrespectful counties in the country. This caused a certain amount of alarm and misgiving. At the end of the holiday, full of new raw material, I would be on my way back to Glasgow, when my mother's parting words would be: 'Now you be careful what you go writing in the Glasgow Herald. Everybody here knows who you are, and where you got these stories from.'

She certainly had a point, and, though so far as I heard these chickens did not come to roost, I did have one narrow escape. It was a feature of Caithness anecdotage, which made as much of an old story as of a new one, that it was never too precise about dates.

There was a spell when the police became unexpectedly industrious about after-hours drinking, a subject on which the local constables tended to be tolerant. The operation was masterminded from Wick, whence in the late evening motorised raiding parties were sent out to make snap visits to the hostelries in the county. It was going on the witching hour one Saturday night when the commando screeched to a halt and burst in upon the saloon bar of the Portland Hotel at Lybster, and began taking names and addresses from the considerable company there assembled. The task was nearly completed, and the policemen were putting away their notebooks, when they noticed one carouser who had been overlooked. He was stretched peacefully on the carpet beneath one of the bigger tables; and when the sergeant of police stepped forward and stirred him, quite gently, with the toe of a regulation boot, he turned comfortably to the touch, and murmered: 'Ah'll jist hae the same as the rest o' ye.'

I absorbed this as a reminiscence, one of the timeless stories of the place, and filed it away in the holiday repertoire. And within a couple of days of my return I used it as the tailpiece to the daily column that I was then writing on the leader page of the Glasgow Herald. It was with some alarm that I learned (by telephone from my equally worried mother) that I had anticipated by a full day the appearance of the accused in Wick Sheriff Court. Happily I was not pursued for contempt of court — of which I was clearly guilty — but thereafter, when I sat at the feet of the story-teller by the kitchen door, I was always careful to ask, 'And when exactly did this happen?'

I was on safer ground with Mr Murray, the autocratic head gardener to the Duke of Portland at Langwell, who did not in the least mind being reported, even to the point of repeating the pay-off line to make sure that I had got it right. In the season, the gardens at Langwell were open to the public, and it was there one day that he came across two mature women gazing rapt and in some doubt at a tree growing against a southfacing wall. At last one of them, noticing and recognising him, asked, 'Will ye tell me; just what kind o' a tree is that?'

'It's a fig tree. There's a label on it.'

Upon which, turning to her companion, she said, 'Did ye hear him? Mind ye, I'd 'a thocht the leaves would be bigger nor that.'

———— * ————

'May I never move,' said my Uncle James, Aunt Maggie's youngest brother, who was addicted to avowals of the kind, 'may I never move, if I was not as sober as I never was before on a Thurso sale day. Ask your aunt.' The look which I intercepted on that occasion stifled the inquiry, and my Cousin William, who had no manners, made a sound like tearing sandpaper. But with a certain injured defiance James went on. 'And it's the God's truth I'm telling you. Mind you, it's no that we werna feeling good, for barring once at Forsinard, and that was ten years ago, I have not had such prices for my cast ewes.

'We were all friendly enough in the back bar, and quiet, too, except for that clouther of a cousin of yours, who was bragging so much about a puckle eeshan craturs of lambs he spoon fed through the spring. You know what it was like as well as I do myself. All the chiels from the hills were there, some of them that hadn't been out for months. We were sitting round the tables in the sitting-room having our crack, and the dogs were lying peaceful like round our feet. My Ben only was making a groan now and again. But he had had a bit of difference with yon wild black bitch from Backlass and had lost the half of an ear. The rest was a low sort of a murmur except when one would roar for a full glass. There wasn't but one bit of an argument, about the worth of a cross stot; and by faith it looked they would come to blows till the dogs joined in. By the time we had cursed them quiet the stot business was forgotten.

'I tell you that just to show what an ordinary evening it was. And there was Gordon sitting mum in a corner with ae foot tucked well under him. He had a schooner in his hand, and now and again he'd put the glass down and twitter a wee bittie on his chanter, low kind. But about ten o'clock a foggy, far-away look came intil his eye, and he yoked the chanter back in the inside pocket of his heather-mixture plus-four jacket. His head went back till we could see the three black hairs that he keeps on his Adam's apple, and then we heard him singing softly, "I to the hills will lift mine eyes" — aye, and putting out the line too.

'As sure as I'm here that made us kind of thoughtful, and it seemed to come over us all at once that we'd half-promised to be home betimes, and anyway the serving lassie was beginning to mutter about closing up. Beelie said, "Weel, chiels, who's for the road?"

I said, "So what?"

My Uncle James said, "Will ye no have patience, man?"

And my Cousin William said, 'Let the auld blether be, he's doing fine.'

My Uncle James went on, 'It was black out in the yard and it was raining, and your cousin, who is lazy and a liar, said there was no carbide in his bicycle lamp, and he was damned if he was going to push it twenty miles in the dark. That was an idea that just needed the starting, and you'd be surprised how quick the rest of them discovered flat tyres and bad lamps. Ye see they knew well enough that Gordon had his car with him, and that he never passed a man or a beast on the road yet but he offered them a lift.

'It is not what ye'd call exactly a limousine. A sports model. Open, with a hood, only the hood has been since long stopping a big hole in the byre roof that was made when a March storm went off with half the thatch. It has, I think, sixteen horse power, and one day in the back-end the petrol tank at the back fell off, so for about six months he had been running over Caithness with a temporary tank, which lay on the back seat and had been connected up by himself. I think the insurance man has been at him since.

'But when men are wanting their bed they can do a deal of right close packing, and Gordon was willing. Well, without a word of a lie we set off for home with Beelie, William, and Macphee sitting with Gordon in the front: and in the back myself, and a gappach chiel whose name I canna mind; and a surfaceman from Altnabreac, four dogs, and three bicycles, and two wedder lambs I got for five shillings each — and Kenny.

'Kenny — you know his place, away up in below Morven and as far from civilisation as if it was at the North Pole? Kenny had been having a great day. He was cleaner than ever I saw him before. He wasn't exactly clean-shaven, but it looked as if Bella had been at his beard with a scissor, and it was only if you looked close you could see the sharn on his boots. He would ride home if it was the last thing he did. So there he was sitting between a dog and a lamb and a bicycle on the petrol tank with his legs sticking out over the side like a binder.

'It was good going. Not fast mind ye; just a nice hand pace. Sedate you might say. And there's no call to believe that Smith at Harpsdale if he tells you he saw us going by at fifty miles and us singing ,"Oh, will you go love and leave me noo," with the surfaceman beating Kenny on the brow with his closed fist and roaring, "Give her line, boy: give her line."

'It was dark and he couldn't see, and besides it was myself that was beating time.

'All went merrily as a marriage bell, as you might say, until we were nearly on the home stretch. By that time we were off the made roads and well into the hills about five miles from Kenny's place. We were taking the corner at Loch More fairly canny, but for some reason which we never quite got out of him Gordon mistook a bit of the hill for the track and ran her fair into the ditch. She did three somersaults.'

I said, 'Three?'

'Well, at least two.'

'One,' said my Cousin William coldly. 'But it is true that she landed on her side and threw us all out.'

'Is it you that's telling this,' observed my Uncle James with great dignity. 'If so. . . .'

'Na, na, on ye go,' says William.

'Well then,' Uncle James continued, 'we have now agreed that the motor was lying on its side in the ditch. It was empty. And all the contents were scattered like the seed of the wicked.

'We recovered ourselves, more or less, and set about righting the car, which was easy, and finding the sheep and pacifying the dogs, which was not easy. Kenny had not been helping, but we did not think much of that, because he's funny about lifting his hand unless there's a glass in it.

'At last when things seemed about right again we noticed that Kenny was missing. We looked, and saw him in a whin. Of course we thought he had been skulking, and if it wasn't for your aunt sitting there with her ears open for a wrong word, I'd tell you what we said. But he just groaned and said his legs were sore. It was wearing late, so we did not wait to argue, but histed him into the car and away again. There was a bit more singing and temping, but Kenny seemed kind of thoughtful, cowning a bittie, but not loud. It just seemed he was suddenly terrible sober. When we got to his road-end he still couldn't walk; but we had still miles to go and could not be waiting just for the sake of a bruise or two. So we lifted him down and sat him up against his gatepost in the heather, and sounded the horn for his women-folk. We knew to make off fast when we saw the door opening.'

'And that was that,' I said, a little disappointed at the repetition of a somewhat familiar episode.

'Well, not quite,' says my Uncle James. 'We did not hear anything for upwards of two months. You know how sometimes we lose touch with the ones far up the hills.

'One day Beelie came in past with his face just full of a good story. He started to speak, and then choked and went rolling about the kitchen floor with the laughter; and there wasn't a sensible word came out of him till your Cousin William had pelted him across the head with a bag of peat meals.

'Between roars he said he had gone up the hills with a rifle after deer and came in on Kenny's place from the back. He was the first visitor since the sale day.

'Bella was at the hay, and when he was passing Beelie calls, "How's Kenny?"

'That was too much for her. She sat down on a cole hugging the fork and rocked herself back and fore, laughing. Then she says, "Ye better go an' see for yersel."

'So Beelie went down to the cottage, and gave a dirl to the door. After a whilie it opened, slow kind; but he couldna see a soul. The place was as dark as it always is and full o' smoke. He went to go in to the kitchen and tripped over the queerest thing ever he saw. It came just aboot up to his knees.

'It was Kenny himsel', as black as a piece of the deevil; and a queer like shape, like one of yon seals, and soot was hanging on his whiskers. His hands and arms were black too, and he was in grand form.

'"Come awa in," he says. And when Beelie got him in the light in the middle of the kitchen floor he saw that he was humphing himself along on his hands with a queer hirpling shuffle and dragging behind him an end like a tail. Beelie thought of the seal because he was wearing an old black petticoat of Bella's.

'Kenny told him his legs hadn't been much use since after that night. He showed them to Beelie, and man, they were an awful funny shape. They spread out from the knees and wouldn't hold him. He'd been managing some odd jobbies like milkin' the cow, but as usual, the women had been doing the work.

'It seems,' said my Uncle James, 'that after he was left at the gate Kenny roared till the women came out for him. They reached their own conclusions and carried him into the house. He was in the way of taking to his bed for a day or two after a jaunt to town, so they never thought his legs were broken. And they didn't notice how long he was in getting up; and when he did they thought he was right funny and kept on saying it till he began to see the joke himself. The strange thing is that the legs had been broken both in the same place, and they set themselves at an angle of about 45 degrees.

'Your Aunt gave Beelie that bit of her mind that she usually saves for myself, and sent for the doctor. And the next we saw was Kenny riding past our place in state, jeering and waving to all his friends through the swinging open door of an ambulance.'

I had the last chapter from the local doctor. Apparently they had to break his legs and set them again; but he had a grand time in the hospital.

Unfortunately I cannot repeat what he is reported to have said to the sister and the matron when they argued that he might be within his rights in smoking black twist in bed, but that since there were two occupied beds intervening he must stop spitting into the fireplace.

—— * ——

I have a special, but unwearable, pair of shoes. They are a trophy. They are excellent shoes. They weigh three and a half pounds each, and if I did not know they came from Dunbeath I would say they were made of very old rhinoceros hide, lurks and all. I acquired them on a visit to some of my nearest and dearest in Caithness.

In our family theft is not recognised as an offence; individually we enjoy clear consciences and a sense of common ownership. This means that it is the responsibility of each member of the clan to keep an eye on his own possessions, and he must blame himself for what he loses. There are no recriminations. You win back what you can.

This point of view is enshrined and sanctioned in the ancient convention of 'First out, best dressed.'

We inherited the habit of mind from our mother's generation of ten brothers and sisters who claimed not only one another's clothing when it fitted but also such other equipment as trinkets, harness, and books of salmon flies. The ebb and flow of gear grew wider as they became the commanding officers of independent companies of nephews and nieces, and the traffic, like a progressive multiple store, began to extend from under one roof to several.

At the same time a certain restraint of trade was imposed by the presence in some of the new headquarters of an alien and un-sympathetic assistant camp commandant, so that smuggling tended to confine itself to articles that had been in circulation since the days of the common roof. Wives and husbands with household goods and goods of their own had an inhibiting narrowness of mind in the matter of mine and thine.

The effect of this was to establish a diminishing number of things in general exchange through two generations: and an increasing number of things in limited circulation within each of the distinct units. Thus while I might compete with my cousins John and William for the possession by stealth of the fishing rod which had been our grandfather's, there would have been real trouble if I had attempted to purloin the mandoline which belonged to their mother.

The question of intrinsic value or usefulness does not enter into the calculations of the tribal contrabandist. The game is played for its own sake, and the pieces in themselves have no more significance than the pawns on a chessboard.

It is now a matter of some eighty years since the senior generation took to this pilfering. At its height, just after the turn of the century, there must have been a great variety of trade goods, but by the time I entered the traffic with my two brothers the range had been considerably reduced. We had heard of gaffs and guns, but long before our day they had been removed from circulation by some strong-minded relative-in-law, and had become inviolable in one or other of the households that had passed from our control.

These original tokens in fact had so dwindled in recent years that at the last count there remained but two: a silver and leather whisky flask with a detachable cup, and a stag's horn snuff box: both of which I am happy to say are now in my possession and, I think, sufficiently well guarded to remain there.

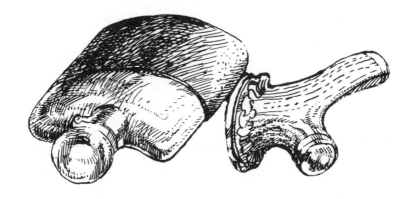

The flask belonged to our grandfather. The snuff box is dated 1830, and appears to be a relic of an even earlier system of family exchange, for it bears the name of a now remote kinsman, Thomas Gunn, Thurso. My mother remembered it standing on a mantelpiece at Westerdale. She could not say when it was first lost sight of.

Many years ago my father, who was never possession proud, returning south from a winter holiday in Caithness, was prevailed upon by my grandmother to take the flask with him. She was a great believer in the sovereign properties of a drop of spirits against the rigours of a journey on the old Highland Line.

The flask, in which at that time I had no practical interest, remained lying about in our house for some months. But it was missed shortly after a visit we had had from Uncle George and Aunt Maggie. The loss was mentioned without malice or ill-will. When the summer came round I spent the holidays with them at Fearn, where family worship twice a day and three services, two English and one Gaelic, on Sunday, did not seduce my attention from the flask. When school resumed in September the flask was back with us in Glasgow.

Again nothing was said, but in the course of the succeeding twenty years the flask made the same journey as many times, with an occasional diversion back to Westerdale.

I particularly remember one of these removals. Once again I was on my way back to Glasgow and had packed my case. The last thing that went in was the flask. In the morning we were waiting for the carrier to come for the luggage when Aunt Maggie came downstairs waving a jacket, which I had forgotten to pack, and saying, 'Stop you, I'll just put it in on the top of your case.'

Was I not fluent the way I persuaded her that it would probably be cold on the train and that it would be more convenient if I would just carry the jacket over my arm?

That anxiety was not founded in any sense of guilt or on any delusion that the action would be considered blameworthy. I was merely afraid of letting the side down by breaking the only rule of the game — that the transfer should be undetected. Aunt Maggie might have removed the booty or she might have ignored it. But either way I would have had to call that round lost.

The snuff-box in its day made longer journeys, having once gone to Canada. I think it must have come back from there about 1924. That was the year that Uncle George went on a preaching trip to the Free Churches in Canada. No one had seen the snuff-box since 1913, and it turned up again only when I fell heir to the desk which was presented to Uncle George by the Young People of Tolsta when he left Stornoway for the mainland in 1910. I feel that I may now declare the snuff-box out of circulation for it has come to me legitimately along with the two dozen note-books of sermons among which it was hidden in the top drawer of the desk.

In my own generation we made the game a little more difficult by the tacit adoption of a new rule. There was still no chiding, but when our young brother William visited either of us, his siblings, we were solicitous and helpful at his departure. And he on his part did not resent it when we opened his luggage at the last minute, any more than we protested when on our visits to him he made a point of pressing us to settle down for a nice cup of tea while he hurried off with our suitcase to the station half an hour before we ourselves needed to be setting out.

We knew what to expect and made other arrangements. There was, for instance, the case of the war souvenir. I was much interested once, in 1947, in a Nazi dagger of fine workmanship and design. It did not go into the case, but into an inside pocket. I never heard a hint that it had been missed. It is a subject we never discussed. All I know is that I have not got it any more and that the last time I saw it it was back in the place that I stole it from. But one of the daughters was watching it.

In our own restricted circle of three brothers and three cousins there were for many years in circulation a pair of binoculars, an old telescope, a box of oil paints that belonged to our father, a Haenel air-pistol, and this pair of shoes — which have solid iron-work on the soles and feel as if they had been forged, uppers and all, by the Dunbeath blacksmith.

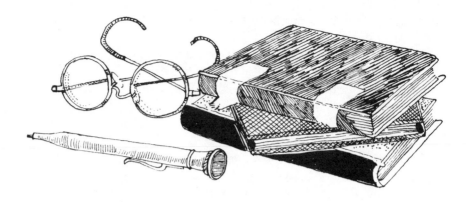

CHAPTER NINE

HURRICANES IN THE PULPIT

WHEN Uncle George was a child at the school in Lybster he used to climb up on the dyke and preach sermons to his classmates. Even in those days his delivery was said to be good and his material strong. This early training also gave him a sense of balance which was still with him when, forty years later, I used to watch him pacing the wide pulpit of the Free Church at Fearn like the captain on the bridge of a ship in a hurricane. Sometimes you could even see him dashing the spray from his eyes as he peered over the book-board into the spiritual mirk that was eternally looming over his congregation.

Uncle George's was a splendid pulpit for a preacher of his restlessness. It had a floor space of five paces in each direction, with a long, twisted, brass holder for a paraffin lamp on each of the two forward corners. These added to the nautical effect, for, when he reached one of them and put his hand high on it to support him as he swung round and leaned over the rail to force a point of dogma into a somnolent pew, he looked more than ever like a sailor on the Minch, shouting above the storm.

And his discourse came to the congregation, too, in waxing and waning waves for, having made his point to north-east, he would stride away to the south where some of the more prosperous farmers' families were entrenched among their own soft cushions and foot-stools, his voice trailing behind him and conserving its strength to hurl the fear of the Lord, which is the beginning of wisdom, into another compass bearing.

Again, when his line of argument made it necessary for him to beat the Book with his closed fist, he would return to the centre of the pulpit, where he commanded the clock in the front of the gallery (which never went), the main and meeker body of the congregation, and a view of the elders if he leaned well over and looked down. They sat in a semi-circle, within a railing of their own, round the base of the pulpit. Only the precentor remained invisible, for he sat facing the congregation and immediately below the book-board. He took advantage of this privileged position to sleep soundly between the Psalms, in full view of all but the minister. It was not, however, a position of perfect security, for it lay in the line of jetsam from the pulpit, and more than once he was nearly brained in his sleep.

Uncle George had an eloquence that called as its natural accompaniment for practical illustration. He himself had the delusion that in his middle age he had become a man of restraint and mild gestures. One Sunday, to direct our attention to the darkness which invested our spirit, he pointed with one hand to the extinguished lamp on the left side of the pulpit. With the other hand he seized the brass standard and shook it so that the lamp funnel was dislodged and fell to shivers among the feet of the elders. He never missed even an accidental cue, and from that point went on to enlarge on the illustration.

On the way home from church I mentioned the incident as being dramatic and effective. What I said was, 'You fairly wakened them that time. It even roused Aunt Maggie.'

'Ah, but you should have seen me when I was younger,' he answered, and told of an evening service at Onich, where hell, flaming, spluttering, and hot, was one of his headings. Though he dealt with the subject with imagination and feeling he had the exasperated sense that his point was not getting across to a stolid evening congregation. The words pouring from him like brimstone, he slapped his pockets, fumbled in them, and brought out a handful of matches and dropped them on the open Bible. Then he picked up three of them and holding them with their heads together, he put his foot up on the platform chair, and scratched them on the seat of his trousers.

As they burst into flame he cried, 'There, do you see *now* what I mean?' and, hurling them to the floor, tramped them out.

He never went that far in my day, but he still used for his illustrations everything on the pulpit that was not screwed down. Thundering across his quarterdeck with a denunciation, he would heave the heavy chair out of his path, leaving it rocking behind him. Again, he would take the great Bible in his hands and hold it up for the congregation to see. That point made, he forgot it while his mind and eye went on to further commentary, leaving his hands, unwatched, to put the book back. It was an absent-minded gesture that often just missed the place.

There seemed to be a providence that protected the precentor's head. I only once saw a direct hit, and that was when Uncle George, flailing with his spectacles, thrashed the edge of the pulpit so hard that they flew from his hand and hit the drowsy precentor fair on the bald spot.

Though he never consulted an optician in his life, Uncle George never lacked for spectacles. He had them gold rimmed, steel rimmed, horn rimmed; he had them rimless and with thin chains that hung over the ears and he even had a pair with a cord that ran like a roller blind's into a sort of pillbox that was worn on the lapel of the coat. His approach to glasses was unscientific but adequate. If he could see through them then they suited him. He inherited and peered confidently through the spectacles of every parishioner who died. Honest as the day in all other ways, he did not wait for death to give him the spectacles of his relatives and the reverend colleagues who frequently passed a week-end in the manse. He used to get his best haul at Communion time.

I am in no position to pass an opinion on Uncle George's theology, but I have heard that he was unequalled in his day on the Old Testament. I can say only that he was an Evangelical, and an impulsive preacher, who held a low opinion of the doctrine of grace by works, and of the Moderates who accepted it.

This was the term — an echo from the Disruption — which he applied to all members and ministers of the Church of Scotland. And it also encompassed within its single embrace a complete explanation of Sabbath-breaking, ministers who played golf and wore lay clothing off duty, Sunday newspapers, and the compromise, general in the Church of Scotland, which permitted people to use public transport on Sundays. Moderates were the type of people who were content to listen to broadcast religious services.

There were venial sins, and errors of outlook which did not earn me the ebony stick. For these I suffered the severe reprimand, 'You are nothing but a Moderate.'

He also thought much of the pulpit rebuke, though as he grew older he used it with increasing tact.

He used to count the congregation during the first Psalm, and he had a photographic memory for where the blanks occurred among the pews. To these vacant places he would address the threat of an early pastoral visit. Eccentricities in women's fashion he dealt with usually in a general way, and he never, so far as I can recollect, went the length of the Free Presbyterian minister in Glasgow who once dismissed two of his congregation from the gallery to wash their faces, because he said that from the pulpit he could see the lipstick on their mouths. I believe he called it 'paint'.

At the turn of the century Uncle George while still a Free Presbyterian, was inducted to the charge of the Free Presbyterian congregation of Stornoway. It was there that he learned the classical Gaelic of the West, and outgrew the defective idiom of his native Caithness dialect and usage. The Gaelic, he used to tell me, was the ideal language for devotion and vituperation, and he was capable of both.

At that time there was in Stornoway but one substantial firm of hirers, by the name of Henderson, whose horses were (at least in his opinion) notoriously given to falling down.

The Free Presbyterian congregation, while devout and faithful, had its human failings. The young fishermen, for instance, were perhaps too fond of a drink on the Saturday night. Uncle George was no teetotaler and objected not to their drinking but to the hangover which frequently prevented their attendance at the morning service on Sunday. The fault, as he conceived it, was not one of intention, for they always turned up at the evening service. This was a drift, a 'slackness', as he called it, that required correction. And one Sunday evening when he had them in the pews before him, he administered the chastisement, saying — this would be in the Gaelic: 'I am seeing you sitting there in front of me, you young men with your innocent faces and your bloodshot eyes. On the Saturday evening, when it is to the public house you are going, you have on you the wings of the eagle; but on the Sabbath morning, when you should be making for the church, you have on you the legs of Henderson's horses.'

By 'Moderate' measurements, Uncle George's sermons were long. We reckoned that if we left the manse about 10.30 on Sunday morning, and took in both the Gaelic and the English, we would be back for luncheon just before 2 o'clock. The Gaelic service was slightly the longer, possibly because of the time consumed by putting out the line, which doubled the length of each Psalm. At the end of the first service about half of the Gaelic congregation went home, and three of the elders. These were mostly the aged wives from Hilton and two or three old men who, as they used to say, couldn't get the taste off the English. The others sat in their pews for twenty minutes to watch the more pretentious English congregation assemble, which included all the wealthier farmers whose wives and families contended unremittingly to establish an order of precedence.

This depended on the late entrance and that family was always counted the winner that was the last to dispose itself in its pew before Uncle George rose in the pulpit and said, 'Let us worship God.'

Uncle George played no favourites and kept honours even by using his discretion. The full effect required a dignified procession down the aisles, the father leading at a slow march and setting the pace for the wife, family, and guests, who followed in file in order of stature. Sometimes when one family might seem to have been winning so often, Uncle George would wait until the leader was emerging from the shadow of the balcony before he loomed suddenly from behind the book-board and gave the word that started the service and turned the procession into a scutter. This was always salutary. It established the authority of the Church; it gave victory to the runners-up; it was a reminder that all is vanity and such a lesson in humility that one might expect to find that family first in its pew the next Sunday.

Between the services Uncle George went down the back stair from the pulpit into the vestry where he sucked his two raw eggs, adjusted his mind to the other language, and took a final glance at the half-sheet of notepaper on which were written the heads of his English discourse. The paper remained on the vestry table, for among the fairly numerous objects of his despite were ministers who read their sermons.

The length of his sermons — for he would speak for an hour — and the habit of delivering them without notes, committed him to a great deal of preparation, particularly in finding just the tone in which he wanted to hurl his best denunciations, or the great rolling phrases for which he had a fine ear.

He used to try these out on the family, removed a little from the context in which they would reverberate around the ears of the congregation. When Aunt Maggie, who did not like to see me idle, being herself an incorrigible worker, had called me to go and weed the walks or help her to pick the gooseberries, Uncle George, secure in the knowledge that he himself was officially studying, had removed me from my 'no-vell' and sent me through the manse to my duty with the booming injunction to, 'Go to the aunt thou sluggard, consider her ways and be wise.'

At other times he was more gently, more sympathetically, derisive, as on the day when, summoned to go and wash myself and polish my boots so that I might be presentable for an expected visitor, I grumbled, and he murmured, 'Moab is my washpot; upon Edom will I cast out my shoe.'

On Saturday he was immured in the study where he paced all day, preparing two sermons in English and one in Gaelic. He could not give the same oration in both languages, not only because half the Gaelic congregation remained for the English, but also because the subject matter for an emotional Gaelic discourse becomes flat and un-convincing when translated. Through the closed door we could hear the rise and fall of his periods, and every now and again one would detect the same muffled cadence repeated over and over again.

Uncle George had great powers of concentration and an insatiable domestic curiosity. His sense of duty insisted that he give his Saturdays totally to the preparation of his sermons, and in that, with but a single lapse in my knowledge, he never made any concessions. But it irked one as sociable as he to be shut away in his study hearing during the pauses in his monologue the sounds of activity elsewhere in the house. Every now and again he would compromise and break out from his seclusion to investigate, but without losing the thread of his discourse.

He walked among us, through the morning-room, into the kitchen and even out as far as the stable. He did not speak to us, but, remaining detached and inquisitive, went on with his preparation, muttering to himself, sometimes beating an imaginary Book or pointing an accusing finger. Looking Aunt Maggie in the eye, he would say, 'And thirdly....' at the same time as he sniffed what she was cooking or stole some of what she was baking; then casting up his eyes and saying, with heavy sorrow, 'As an ox goeth to the slaughter....' he would wander off, prowling and preaching through the rooms to see what I was doing.

Sometimes he has come upon me sitting fumbling, trying to tie a

cast on a fishing line, and with a friendly light in his eye, but denunciation in his voice, he has elaborated a devastating theory on the
pains of hell at the same time as, taking the tangled line from my
hands, he has tied the necessary fisherman's knot and handed it back
to me.

At other times, if it was near noon, he would intone:

> The lion's young may hungry be,
> And they may lack their food.

And then, his curiosity allayed by his tour of the family, he would
drift back to the study, his voice trailing behind him, questioning,
reproving, explaining, and running lovingly over the good telling
points and the purple passages. The door would bang behind him,
and until a dish was broken or a strange voice heard, or until a smell of
cooking reached him, he would be alone with his sermon and the desk
(which I have inherited) inscribed:

> *Presented to the Rev. George Mackay*
> *by the Young People of Tolsta,*
> *Caolish, Lewis, 1910*

and the library to which he seldom referred.

Uncle George's library, like so many that one finds in manses, was
an imposing façade of commentaries, treatises on the Prophets, and
high-minded odds and ends, such as Murray M'Cheyne and *The Days
of the Fathers in Ross-shire.*

I remember the awe with which one of my less literate cousins
asked, after his death, 'What will become of his library?' and the shock
which I caused by suggesting that a man with a book barrow might
give 10s. for it. Uncle George got most of it at auction sales in Highland
manses for so much a yard. To the main bulk, from which the chalked
'Lot 23' had never been rubbed off, there were added over the years a
set of encyclopaedias, a dictionary, and some respectable secular
accretions with nice bindings. Of these I can remember only the
Essays of Elia and *Sartor Resartus.* But dotted through the shelves,
with which Uncle George never interfered, were signs of the passing
of profane and light-minded visitors. Over a period of many summers
I observed with interest that six volumes of a commentary on Isaiah
were separated from a two-volume interpretation of the Psalms by
The Wrong Mr Wright by Ruby M. Ayres.

There was one Saturday when Uncle George did not come out to
walk among us. We were both alarmed and interested, for the words
that came to us through the study door had a different rhythm and a

different spirit. All day we were hearing strange snatches of personal history spoken with the deepest feeling. It was a new background of martyrdom with which even Aunt Maggie was quite unfamiliar.

We, who knew him to be over sixty, and of an optimistic disposition, distinctly heard him say with a sob:

> My hair is grey but not with years,
> Nor grew it white in a single night
> As men's have grown from sudden fears.

We might have agreed with him that his '. . . legs are bowed but not with toil'. But considered that he was being unfair to himself when he added that they were rusted with a vile repose.

These confessions might have belonged to the dramatic licence which he sometimes permitted himself, but there was no understanding the line that came loudest and most fervently from the room. Not only did he distinctly say, but he repeated at intervals all day, that his father had perished at the stake for the tenets he would not forsake.

His immediate forebears were indeed strong defenders of the faith and would undoubtedly have welcomed martyrdom. But even his grandfather of Clashcraggan, who was known as one of the fathers of the far North, came through the Disruption triumphant and unscathed.

Sunday was an anti-climax. He preached a sermon that we had heard before — a calm, tolerant one, without a threat of the life to come — and not a word about the grey hairs or the perishing on the stake.

When I reproached him with it he confessed that while reaching for his Gaelic dictionary he had lifted by mistake a copy of Byron, and opening it casually had found the place at *The Prisoner of Chillon* and was seduced from his text. He spent the day memorising the poem, and, discovering too late to do anything about it that he had forgotten all about his sermon, he rehearsed an old one.

That was the only time that I can say for certain he took his notes into the pulpit with him — and there were three empty egg-shells in the vestry.

——— * ———

Though he did not read his sermons, Uncle George took copious notes while thinking about them. I have his notebooks, and I wish that from them I could reconstruct the burden of his discourses, which were highly esteemed not only in the Highlands, but also in Canada and Australia, even by such unlikely luminaries as a South Australian Anglican bishop. That would be when he was speaking English.

This, and other econiums, I must take for granted; because I knew Uncle George's prayers better than his sermons. This was the subliminal effect of regular family worship. As for the pulpit dissertation, I was alive only to those hints which indicated that he was directing a personal reproof in a particular direction.

This is a lack which I might have corrected in later life, had I only been able to read his miniscule and hasty handwriting. As it is, with his notebooks before me, I find it impossible, sometimes, to decide whether he was writing in English or in Gaelic — let alone decipher the whole of a single sentence.

It is, of course the price of my own beardless inattention that, having been for so long exposed to the odour of sanctity, so much of its redolence has gone with the wind. I remember Uncle George's gestures, and the sound of his voice, but not his words. My shortcoming (as with Hamlet's King Claudius) was that while *his* words flew up, *my* thoughts remained below.

In those early years what might be described as my control group for comparison was somewhat limited, and my reactions were strictly earthbound. Thus of a young and undeviating minister, whom I have since heard praised for the passion of his eloquence, all that remains with me is that he addressed heaven, or the ceiling, and that his over-developed Adam's apple went up and down like an express elevator. In my day I should have assimilated the gentle exhortations of the regular visiting minister from Kiltearn, but all he has bequeathed to my memory has been the thin, high, squeak of his voice.

In my occasional role as the representative of the manse, in the absence of the minister, I tended to be extremely arrogant and condescending in the presence of the more uncertain student preachers whom I led to the church; and to whom I explained the exiguous amenities of the vestry, and the hidden danger of the second-top step of the secret stairway to the pulpit. I also gave good advice upon the dreadful subject of reading.

And I would finally shake what fragments of self-confidence that remained in him by saying, with malignant concern, 'You are surely not going to be taking that bundle of papers into the pulpit with you.'

Of course none of them would ever admit that it was his sermon he had in his hand, and that he intended to read it under the cover of the great pulpit Bible.

'Just notes,' he would say. 'The heads, you know, to keep me in mind of the order of the discourse.'

If the young man had been discreet enough to treat me with the comradely deference which I always felt I deserved, I would let him off lightly, merely saying: 'Well, you had better just be sure that you don't let old Uisdean Macangus see you turning the pages. You watch him. He's the elder with the bushy eyebrows and the big brown snuff handkerchief.'

But woe betide any of them who (albeit just practising) had presumed, either at breakfast, or on the walk to church, to examine my own state of grace. For such I saved my parthian shot for the post-service progress back to the manse: 'You read your sermon. Everybody noticed it. The minister will be home tomorrow. He doesn't like that sort of thing, you know. The last supply we had who read his sermon has never been asked back.'

—— * ——

Uisdean Macangus was the senior Gaelic elder, an aged, devout, and stern little fisherman from Hilton. He was one of those who did not stay for the English, and I always had the feeling that he considered worship in that language a frivolity. He wore a skipped cap and a reefer jacket and a double-breasted waistcoat with lapels on it, and slightly bell-bottomed trousers. His hands were knotty and dark-tanned on the backs and pale and pink on the palms and the inside of the fingers from a life-time of salt water and baiting his lines. The gnawed mouthpiece of his pipe stuck out from the lower left-hand pocket of his waistcoat, and, heavy smoker though he was, it remained there every Sabbath until he was a measured one hundred paces away from the church door.

Behind the church a narrow, dusty path led as a short-cut across the fields to the fishing villages. The figures on it looked black and slow, and seemed to have a staggering, remorseless determination about them that was lacking in the English congregation, who went in for coloured hats and, when they were not riding in gigs or traps or motor cars, walked on a summer's day with a briskness and a conscious flirt of the skirt and a sense of parade. The Gaelic con-gregation were much graver, for they came almost entirely from Hilton and Balintore and lived within the patriarchal influence of the elders.

Often when we came out from the English and I was walking with Uncle George we would stop at the church gate to talk with some young farm servant. If he was going in the same direction we might fall into step with him, and he would be embarrassed and uneasy as if there was something on his conscience that made it difficult for him to speak with the minister. This used to worry Uncle George. But he was unobservant and did not know, as I did, that the young man's discomfort was caused by the lit cigarette end that he was trying to conceal in the palm of his hand. There were no such deceits or need for concealment with the Gaelic speakers. Uisdean saw to that, for his word and his discipline were harder even than the minister's.

In the pause between services, while Uncle George was in the vestry sucking his raw eggs and changing his language, you might stand in the main door and watch the people on the path to Hilton who looked like ants or like a picture of the Yukon Trail. Then, over the fence beside a dip in the path, you could see floating up a puff of blue smoke, and then another and another. Uisdean had paced his hundred yards.

There were times when Uncle George was away that the 'supply' did not have the Gaelic. Then Uisdean, with a terrifying humility, would conduct the service, and would wait with obvious resignation through the English so that he might afterwards give some account of the worship to the visiting minister. This was, of course, a formality because Uisdean professed to speak no English, and had the minister had the Gaelic he would have preached himself. Once or twice I have myself acted as interpreter between Uisdean and Professor John MacLeod, without transmitting much in the way of text or theological argument, since my own Gaelic at that time consisted in an ability to count up to ten, and a knowledge of the words for a wet day, a warm day, a fine day, and good-bye.

But both always seemed perfectly satisfied with the exchange. Uisdean would turn away on to the Hilton path and have his smoke, while Professor MacLeod and myself would carry on towards the manse, and, if we felt ourself safe from the more censorious eyes of the congregation, would play 'sodgers' with the long grasses plucked from the roadside. It was not every Free Church minister you could do that with.

The elders, in both languages, were unmistakably of the elect. There were unforgiving eyes among them, and damned disinheriting countenances. They sat, removed, within the railed enclosure surrounding the pulpit, like a semi-circle of Whistler's Carlyles. If the minister, either in prayer or in sermon, said anything worthy of an 'Amen' or a solemn 'Aye, aye', theirs was the privilege of intoning it first. If anyone in the pews presumed even to sigh out of turn, six stern pairs of hooded eyes would stare the interrupter into silence. Even Aunt Maggie never uttered a sound except when she was dominating the praise, but that may have been because she was asleep.

Only the aged and godly 'wifies' from the villages were beyond and above such discipline. Happed in their black clothes and under their widow's bonnets, they rocked themselves to the rhythm of the preacher's voice, reacting as much to the sound as to the sense of his words, and murmuring almost without pause 'shay-shay' ('Is-e, Is-e' in the Gaelic). They were not so noticeable in the wider reaches of the church as at the evening service in the school at Hilton, when Uncle George preached from the teacher's high desk, and they sat, wide and flowing with their hands folded on their laps in the front row of low infants' seats.

I got on famously with the wifies, who used to call me the 'meenister's boay', and kept me supplied with pan drops, which, with an enormous heching and wheezing, they brought out one at a time from the pocket in their stiff black petticoats.

Those school meetings were always crowded, for they were often half-and-half Gaelic and English and commanded the attendance of both congregations. The younger men would sit in the window sills, and the middle-aged and douce would adjust their knees as best they could in the forms for the older pupils. Then there would be the wifies down in the front, and a chair beside the desk for Aunt Maggie to sit in with her back to the blackboard.

There was seldom a chair for me, and I would squat at Uncle George's feet, growing more and more restless as the sermon went on, and sometimes creating a diversion by becoming too engrossed in some private game as digging the dirt out of the cracks in the floorboards. Then Uncle George would quietly stir me to attention with his foot. There would be a rustle when an old woman was turning up her outer skirt to get at her petticoat pocket. Then there would be a nudging as a pan drop was passed from hand to hand till it reached the wifie nearest to me, and she would pass it over to me, hot, slightly melted, with a faint odour of camphor clinging to it. They never scowled, the wifies, like the elders, but with all their keening were placid and understanding.

I knew them well outside of public worship because I went visiting with Uncle George. We used to reach the manse in the evening waterlogged and crippled, for we had tea, and Uncle George put up a word, in every house. That meant a lot of kneeling and all the fisher cottages had flagstone floors. We had tea in every house but Maggie Houston's. One half of her but-and-ben was a sweetie shop. She would say, 'I'm thinking that I saw Kirstag giving you on Sabbath all the pan drops that you would be wanting for a week, but if you can say me "I would like a puckle black-stripe balls" in the Gaelic I'll maybe give you something better than a cup of tea.'

I was always word perfect, for I used to rehearse it with Uncle George on the way up to her door.

Uncle George's was the only Gaelic I trusted. That was because I was once down alone at the pier at Balintore watching the boats coming in and fell in with some young fishermen (Uncle George said they must have been Moderates) who tried some Gaelic on me. I had a quick ear. They made me repeat the phrase over and over again, and then said, 'Now away you and say that to the minister.'

That was the only time I suffered the ebony cane without knowing exactly— that is, word for word— what I was getting it for, but it made me wary of casual Gaelic.

There was a time when the elders took snuff. The mull appeared when the minister came to his second main heading. It passed from Hugh Mackay on the right round the enclosure until it made the full

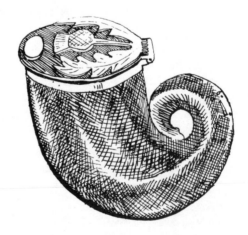

circle to the precentor, sitting directly under the book-board. It was a smooth, undistracting passage. They did not take their eyes off the preacher's face, but each, when his turn came, took the mull from his neighbour, and in his own way, ladled the snuff into his nose. Some of them took it from between their fingers, another put it in a little heap on the back of his hand and sniffed it up, others used the horn spoon. But they never missed a word. Then, as if the pulpit were running up a signal the snuff handkerchiefs would appear in rotation, great squares of brown and red, in which beards and moustaches were briefly lost, but over which the eyes stared, unwinking. But one day there came a new elder, a younger man with a tender nose, and he sneezed, and thereafter, like Uisdean's tobacco pipe, the snuff was banished beyond the hundred yards perimeter of the church.

Only Uisdean of the elders officiated on special occasions in the church. The others had their hour at the Wednesday prayer meeting, where they prayed in turn according to their seniority and saintliness, and might now and again take a shot at expounding. They were all fluent and could go twenty minutes without faltering, and they paid Uncle George the compliment of modelling their prayers on his, in which they, like myself, were nearly word-perfect. There were certain of the more allusive passages which they had not quite properly picked up, and which to a cynic might suggest that they did not always understand everything that they heard and memorised. But I was not cynical, nor was their 'beloved pasture' whom they never failed to remember when they put up a word.

—— * ——

In the Free Church there is no nonsense with the wee red velvet bag that makes it easy for the worshipper who has discovered that he has only a half-crown and a penny.

There is a plate at the outside door, and two impassive elders stand guard over it, one on either side. Sometimes they give a slight nod to the good contributors to the Sustentation Fund; but mostly they just stare with a becoming gravity into the middle distance. They also know exactly how much each member of the congregation has left in the plate. I think that is a special talent passed on from father to son under an oath of secrecy, like the horseman's word.

It was my privilege, arriving under the eye of Aunt Maggie, to enter the church by the vestry door. But once we had taken our place I was given our sixpences and had to trot off down the right-hand aisle against the stream of traffic, to the front lobby and drop them in the plate. This used to strike me as an unnecessary demonstration, because I took it for granted that what the guardian elders did before they reappeared after the first prayer was to take the plate round to the vestry and just empty it into Aunt Maggie's handbag. With my kinsfolk's interest at heart I tried to linger by the plate and, by examining every contribution, shame the congregation into giving more freely. This, however, was not encouraged by the elders who would whisper that it did not look right for me to be hanging about, and they would shoo me back to my place in the manse seat. I learned in time that there was a treasurer who looked after the money and sent it off to Edinburgh. This, I thought, was unfair, and I never fully understood why Aunt Maggie and myself should be expected to pay too, particularly when the elders gave no sign of realising the nobility of our gesture.

I was not alone in this sense of non-recognition.

I once knew a prosperous and godly publican in Aberdeen, and he was most conscious of both his godliness and his prosperity. One Sunday his sense of obligation to the Church was particularly active. He walked before me up the steps to the door and the plate, and the elders stood expressionless like the stone guardians at the entrance to Pharaohs' tombs.

With a flourish the good man dived into his breast pocket and drew out a thick wallet. The elders stared straight ahead. He rustled his thumb over a plump wad and carefully chose a fiver. The elders' minds and eyes were on higher things. He coughed a little and reached out, dropping the note from the height of about a foot on to the plate. One elder nodded to the minister's wife, who was coming up the steps; the other was looking at a cobweb in the top left-hand corner of the door. The final gesture of the good and prosperous man was one of utter defeat. He shook the more impassive of the two by the arm and said: 'Here, Geordie, min; will ye jist pit something on the tap o' that te keep it fae flying awa'?'

—— * ——

Regrettably, while no doubt for the best of reasons, ministers tell lies. This is called 'illustrative material' and even Uncle George at least once sinned to the extent that I was obliged to remind him of the Ninth Commandment (you see, when the occasion was ripe, I knew my stuff). That was a Sabbath when the minister, preaching against loose and profane language, stated for a fact that he had walked home on the Saturday night behind three young men whose every second word had been an oath.

I was then too young and hypocritical to have any tolerance for dramatic licence; and I had to tell him that he had been speaking downright lies, for, as he well knew, I had been near him all the previous day, when he had left his study only to eat his meals.

Uncle George's delivery, and his imagery were modelled upon his great exemplar, Disruption Chalmers, the father of the uncorrupted Free Church, of whose preaching it was written:

'At first there is nothing to make one suspect what riches are in store. But then with what tenfold richness does this preliminary curtain make the glories of his eloquence to shine forth, when the heated spirit at length flings from its fetters, and bursts out, elate and rejoicing in the full splendour of its disimprisoned wings.'

I write of the days before days of electronic aid — and (who knows?) teleprompts, or of microphones on the bookboard; but there is still sufficient resonance in my ears to assert that in the matter of voice projection Uncle George had nothing to learn from the noted Dr Black of Cairneyhill, who while preaching in the open air, could be heard, without a wordmissed, at a distance of over two miles. The reporter of that tour-de-force added: 'The preacher has, perhaps, never been surpassed for distinct speaking and a clear voice; and the wind, which was steady and moderate came against the direction of the sound.'

It took a clear conscience to sit composedly down-wind of the Wee Free minister of Fearn.

—— * ——

Although I never pretended to understand Uncle George's sermons, I was at least word perfect in his prayers. It is possible that I took his allusions, and interpreted the snatches of Biblical quotation on which they were built up, too literally. While praying at family worship he referred at least once a day to the 'well that has been opened for sin and for uncleanness', and of this I had the clearest architectural picture, even down to the bucket and the rope and the winding gear. The equally frequent appeal to be 'tied up in the bundle of life', which I later, in the course of reading verse about, discovered were the words of the Prophet Samuel, evoked only a picture of Bessie the servant gathering faggots in the wood for the kitchen fire.

This was an incitement to inattention, for, with the possible exception of Aunt Maggie who had always something serious and domestic to concentrate on, we had the habit of letting our minds wander during the longer prayers. Thus the bundle of life suggested sticks, and sticks the kitchen fire, and the kitchen fire was always smoking and from that point on the drone of Uncle George's voice might well be no more than a soporific accompaniment to a step by step reconstruction of the sweeping of a chimney.

My complete familiarity with the prayers was only to be expected for we took the Books twice a day, immediately after breakfast and before bedtime, and I accompanied him on most of his pastoral visits, when he would put up a word in as many as a dozen houses in the course of an afternoon. He fell inevitably into habits of expression so that I just needed to hear one familiar word to be able to fill in for myself the dozen which would follow it.

The grace, too, was stereotyped, varying in length according to the presence of visitors, and the extent and quality of the repast. It could, indeed, be extremely curt on those washing days when the midday meal might be something frugal, like boiled potatoes and milk. On such a day Uncle George would say, 'Grant us Thy blessing with these' pause . . . 'mercies. Amen.'

The order of service at worship was unchangeable. We sang our way through the Psalms, indulging to the full our common preference for Barrow, Covenanters, Stroudwater, and Stornoway. Uncle George, having given the lead, resigned the grace-notes to Aunt Maggie, and the rest of us ploughed our way with dogged humility through the tune.

In the evening we read verse about from the New Testament; in the morning from the Old. The only compromise was the skipping of some of the genealogical tables in Genesis, and we pronounced the proper names as they seemed best to us. We probably derived more instruction from the lesson on those rare occasions when there was a train to catch and Uncle George read the whole chapter himself. The servant, always referred to as 'the girl', and those of us who were children were seldom very fluent at the reading, but were expert in the sharp practice of counting ahead, and rehearsing, while the others were reading, the verses that would fall to us. This spared us the humiliation of stumbling too badly, but it left us with little sense of the continuity of the chapter.

Then we turned round and knelt at our chairs while Uncle George said his prayer. This might last anything from five minutes to half an hour, while we weaker vessels drifted into vague reflections, or into secret games of patience. Easy-chairs and high-backed chairs each had their particular advantages. The high-backed chair was not so comfortable, but it was also less secluded, and, peering through the interstices in the woodwork, one could take unobtrusive observations on the room and on the attitudes of the others. Little things which in the ordinary scurry of activity went unnoticed became fascinating and delightful. You watched a coal teetering on the bars of the grate, and waited to see out of the corner of your eye how many would start when it fell. You made little optical tests, like seeing how many titles of books in the bookcase you could read without moving your head. Or there was the simple pleasure to be had in seeing that Uncle George knelt with his toes bent back so that his slippers stuck out at an angle exposing the heel of a sock in which there was a big round hole. That was the sort of thing that Aunt Maggie would notice, too, for in the very act of rising from her knees she would be issuing her orders to the maid, and instructing the minister to go straight away and change his socks.

It did not do, however, to catch the eye of any of the fellow-sinners, for Aunt Maggie was watchful, and though she could not identify inattention from a faraway look in an open eye, she was deadly in recognising intercommunication or collaboration.

The best position was facing an open window on a summer's morning. Then one could watch the pigeons and the crows, and keep an informed eye on the traffic passing on the high road.

The easy-chair called for a different, a more private and personal diversion. Sometimes you just burrowed your head into the three planes of an upholstered corner, and after adjusting it to a position where it was possible to breathe easily, went into a light doze. But that was usually for the evening after a long tiring day. More often I would be wakeful and in the mood to trace out the pattern of the tapestry and count the blue threads, or to use the design for an intricate mental game resembling snakes and ladders. There were some easy chairs with wide deep arms that provided a complete retreat, and these were most exciting when they had no loose covers. With elbows and arms safely screened from any general view I have had many thrilling and rewarding treasure-hunts down the back and sides of the upholstery. I found pocket-knives, spectacles, screwdrivers, hundreds of pins, dozens of knitting needles, and many trinkets. The difficulty lay in transferring these undetected from the seat of the chair to the pocket.

These adventures in inattention were insignificant compared with the more constructive idleness of two of Aunt Maggie's younger brothers. Once at worship in my grandfather's house, they miscalculated the length of time that a visiting good man would pray, and when the family and guests rose after an unexpected 'Amen' the two boys were discovered, back to back, standing on their heads on the hearth rug. It was Uncle Dan, who was older, and who, I think, envied them their misdemeanour, who told me of that incident, adding, 'By faith, they got an awful lundering for that one.'

The more common embarrassments in a big family were the figures who remained scattered around the room still kneeling asleep at their chairs after the rest had reached their feet.

In the manse, as in my grandfather's house, guests of known eloquence, whether they were ministers or laymen, had the privilege of praying. This worked well where there was but one, or where the status was clear as between an old preacher and a student. It was among contemporaries of equal sanctity that the host had to steer with discretion, working out an acceptable distribution of graces at meal-times and prayers at worship.

Some used to say that Aunt Maggie was more worldly than Uncle George. She certainly took the responsibility of attempting to cut a prayer short if it overran an urgent earthly time-table. I can remember her tugging quietly at Uncle George's coat-tail while a man in a gig sat outside the door looking at his watch and making signs through the window, as he waited to take us and our luggage to the railway station. But she might as well have been trying to stop the tide for all the attention that she commanded.

This suggests in Uncle George a total removal from any awareness of his surroundings, which is not altogether true. One morning before breakfast Aunt Maggie made a milk pudding which she set to cool on the sill of the open diningroom window. After breakfast Uncle George pushed back his plate and called for the Books. Ten minutes later, looking up from the place at which she was kneeling Aunt Maggie saw the cat on the window sill, stalking the pudding.

She said 'Pssst', but nothing happened, and the cat came closer to the bowl. Uncle George prayed on.

Then Aunt Maggie said 'Pssst' again, louder. The cat gave no heed and Uncle George continued to pray.

But when she said 'Pssst' a third time Uncle George, without pausing in his supplication, reached down beside his chair and picked up a book, and, as he pitched it with perfect aim at the cat, he said, 'That's worth a dozen "Pssst's".'

He then took up the thread where he left it and finished his prayer as though there had been no interruption.

CHAPTER TEN

THE LANGUAGE OF EDEN

UNCLE GEORGE preferred to preach — and to pray — in the Gaelic. And in Stornoway, which was his first charge, once he had purged his tongue of the inelegancies of the Caithness Gaelic that he had learned at his mother's knee, it was the only language that was demanded of him.

In private conversations he might make the odd concession. I have heard him say: 'They tell me that French is the best language for making love; and I suppose the English is good enough for doing business. But for approaching God Almighty, you will be nearer to Him in Gaelic than in any other language.'

There were, however, purists in his acquaintance, who held that Lewis had not been the ideal place to go to polish up his Gaelic and acquire a proper accent. This apparently was because, a century or so ago, there was an influx of weavers from the East Coast, who, having learned the language, imposed their own tone upon it, with the result that a couple of generations later the folk in and around Stornoway spoke it with a Fife accent.

Gaelic, in fact, is so arrogantly divisive that it is small wonder that it is dying out, as rapidly as each successive Census tots up its melancholy head-count. There is the delusion among the exiguous population of Harris, just the width of a burn away from Lewis, that theirs only is the perfect original tongue. There is a concensus that Ballacuilish Gaelic is gibberish, and that a pure speaker from

Inverness would be hard wrought to follow the native conversation of a man from Islay.

Even in Uncle George's day, when he was a pillar of what was formally known as the Gaelic Free Church, he was fighting a rear-guard action; as he found when, in 1910, he left the islands to preside over a rich agricultural parish in what was by comparison the lush sub-tropical plains of Easter Ross. There the social distinctions that have bedevilled the language, and guaranteed its decline, became patent. Gaelic was a tongue despised in the landward tracts of the parish; a vernacular spoken by the fisherfolk of the seaward villages, a people whom even the humblest of farm servants held to be an inferior consumption-ridden race, and dying out. These, however, were the worshippers upon whom the minister relied for the response to his eloquence.

I never once, in the larger English congregation, heard a passionately approving 'Amen' or 'Halleluja' from the pews; while in those Gaelic services, in which I took the uncomprehending spectator's part, the scene was active with nodding lyart locks and black widow's bonnets, and the air loud with the murmuring which sounded like 'Shay-shay' (but was Is-e, Is-e, 'It is so').

This insidious denigration was apparent in the West Highlands which, even in the days before Lord Leverhulme, had their share of visiting gentry, and the Highlanders themselves were not guiltless of spreading the rot. In common practice the difference between the gentry and the rest was estimated by the generosity of their *vales*. The two comparative coins were the 'golden guinea' and the 'shabby half-crown'.

The measure of this distinction may be found in a delightedly reported experience from Kenneth MacLeod (my favoured source of the more secular Highland lore). He was always a well-dressed person, but not always in his clerical uniform; particularly when he was on his progresses around the islands, collecting the songs and traditions that were beyond the reach of the non-Gaelic-speaking Kennedy-Frasers, who were then assembling and scoring the material for their 'Songs of the Isles'.

On this day in the Uists — or perhaps it was on Barra, where his Auld Kirk writ did not run — he was making his way back to the mainland. And, coming to the head of the jetty where the ferry-boat was moored, he was met by the second boatman, who relieved him of his two suitcases. Kenneth thanked him comprehensively in the native tongue.

109

The man then led him down the jetty to the waiting boat, and, as he handed down the suitcases to the ferryman, he said in a carrying *sotto voce*, 'He is no gentleman. He has the Gaelic.'

'And,' said Kenneth, 'All that was sought from me that day was not the golden guinea, but the shabby half-crown.'

The only divine of another communion to whom Uncle George whole-heartedly deferred was C.H. Spurgeon, the Baptist of the Metropolitan Temple, who had been known to preach to congregations of 24,000. He might well indeed have been a Wee Free, being fervent, anecdotal, sometimes witty, but always relentless in the rooting out of fundamental errors. His picture hung on the wall of the manse study along with the other patriarchs.

Indeed the only apparent defect in Spurgeon was that he did not have the Gaelic. But that was forgiven him; as was his oft-repeated, if somewhat presumptuous pleasantry on the subject.

Towards the end of his ministry, in the course of a preaching pilgrimage, he landed in a Ross-shire Free Church, where he endured two hours of singing (with the precentor putting out the line) and of preaching. The splendour of the language as a vehicle for devotion escaped him, and he said as much to his host minister, who protested, saying:

'But sir, do you not realise that that was the language of our first parents in the Garden of Eden?'

'Then,' replied Spurgeon, 'it is no longer a mystery to me why they were cast out.'

What Spurgeon, of course, could not have been expected to understand was the peculiar and overriding authority of the Gaelic. The importance of the language in this context is illustrated in the circumstantial report of a charge in the remote north west which had been without a minister for many years.

There are in the Church three categories of Highland charges, classified as 'English', 'Gaelic preferred' and 'Gaelic essential', one of these a requirement no longer always easy to fill. This congregation was a 'Gaelic essential'.

The kirk session, distressed at the long vacancy, met to discuss whether, in order to attract a minister, they should petition to be reduced to 'Gaelic preferred'.

'What we want here,' said the senior elder, 'is a man who will preach us the Gospel.'

But he was silenced by the voice of one of his aged brethren, uttering from the back of the hall: 'Never mind the Gospel. What we want here is a man who will preach us the Gaelic.'

——— * ———

Aunt Maggie, who in her own way could be just a shade devious, believed in the native adage that you should aye keep something to yoursel'. She did not speak the Gaelic; and it was well known that she didn't. I myself never remember her speaking a Gaelic word, let alone a sentence.

Now that might seem odd in a practical woman, notably quick in the uptake, whose own mother had the Gaelic as her first language, and who herself had spent ten years and more as the helpmeet of the minister at Stornoway. It was a lack that evoked some supercilious compassion, but she bore that without distress or resentment. The cailleachs of the villages spoke freely among themselves in her presence; and when she chose Aunt Maggie could look convincingly inscrutable. She was, therefore a mine of those most interesting and significant tit-bits of local intelligence which were not allowed to reach the ears of the minister himself.

——— * ———

Still belabouring the language of Eden: we have had our defeats, but also our victories, great and small, and to one of these I am proud to have made my own contribution.

I was irritated by the ineffable superiority that the semi-literate southern English airmen at our camp arrogated to themselves over the primitive natives with whom they came in contact, mainly in the general-store-and-Post Office, in the nearest hamlet of Bayble. Their impolite delight, in tittering public, was to try to reproduce the barbaric sounds of the Gaelic tongue. And there were some prime performers who, truth to tell were hardly intelligible when they spoke in what they imagined to be standard English.

There was, however, in the hamlet an idiot-boy who spoke only Gaelic, but took a fascinated interest in the new and noisy language which had suddenly intruded upon his simple circle. So one day, with the willing help of his bi-lingual playmates, I briefed him. Waiting until the shop was full of impersonating Cockneys and stony-faced villagers, I interrupted the performance, and called upon Johnny, speaking in the Gaelic I had rehearsed, and saying, 'Speak in English, Shonny.'

He was only too happy to oblige, producing a gibberish of animal sounds, which so shocked and enraged the airmen-audience that thereafter they abandoned that particular diversion.

—— * ——

About this time I was also able to report to Uncle George another minor triumph for the Gaelic over the thoroughly inadequate English, even in the alarms and excursions of a totally modern war situation. We had an extreme case of counter-espionage in Lewis, and were called out to take to the heather fully-armed, and if need be to shoot to kill. This was the instruction of our somewhat excitable young American station commander.

The mother of Sondag, who lived in a black-house at Bayble, had a cow. Sondag was a happy, unspoilt child who had never been to the pictures at Stornoway, and, at that time at least, knew nothing of the adventures of Dick Barton. She played the simple games of the country, such as putting a divot on the top of a neighbour's chimney-pot; and in the summer days she guddled in the burn. She feared the dreadful Each Uisge; she fished for cuddies in the abandoned little harbour, and she shared all her ploys with Donaldina, her neighbour and contemporary. Between them they knew every flower in the peat hags above Bayble, and every pretty stone from there to Shader. On the afternoon before Lieutenant Joe

Bunk had us standing to our arms, they had gone off as usual to bring home the cow from the hill, a mild black beast that wandered at will, picking a sweet bite off a moorland that stretched across the Eye Peninsula to the barbed wire entanglements that, in theory, protected the huts where we were engaged in the top-secret task of radio-location.

The lassies were long about it, and the twilight was far spent when the mother, standing impatient at the door with the milk pail at her feet, saw the black cow heave herself over a peat-bank, and come lumbering down the brae to the byre: the little girls running anxiously at her heels.

They came panting to the woman, who did not speak the reproach on her lips when she saw the panic-stricken brightness in their eyes, and the flush on their cheeks.

'Och!' she said, 'Calm you. The Each Uisge will not follow you this far.'

But they stammered that it was something else; something about a stranger who had come up out of the shore, and who had spoken to them in a strange voice.

One of those queer airmen from the camp up the road, opined the mother. But no; this was not the voice of these Englishmen, with which they were all familiar; and besides he was not wearing their uniform.

The black cow bellowed her discomfort, but went unmilked while the woman sent Donaldina home and led her own Sondag down to the shop to put her experience into the more responsible hands of the postmaster and sergeant of the Home Guard.

The substance of Sondag's report was that while looking for the cow, which had wandered farther than usual, they came over to the eastern shore, near Rudha na Greine, and there, under the very shadow of our transmitting pylon, had met a tall man, asking the way to Stornoway airport. Sondag could not describe his features, for she was shy, as are all island children in the presence of strangers. She had hung her head, not daring to look him in the eye; and, instead, had a good look at his boots.

'The toes of them were iron,' she said, 'and the tops of them came up to here,' indicating a point on her own leg well above the ankle. There were stockings on the legs, but more she could not say beyond that the voice had not been unkind. In response to his question she had pointed quickly in the general direction of Stornoway, and then, overcome with emotion, had turned and run away, followed by Donaldina. They had thrown themselves together into a dry peatbank, hiding their heads, and when they looked up the stranger had gone.

This was too much even for a sergeant of Home Guard to deal with on his own, and he called in the military. By the time they had arrived in the person of a security officer and his staff, the interrogation had reached out to embrace a now highly emotional Donaldina.

For all her present hysteria, she had been less bashful than Sondag during the encounter. True, she had not looked the stranger in the face, but she had raised her head high enough to see his jacket, which was of a faded green colour with a buttoned cloth belt. When he turned sideways to follow the line of their fingers pointed towards Stornoway, she noticed that he also wore a narrow haversack with an iron frame.

It was clear that the children, speaking unprompted out of their own ignorance, had described a pair of climbing boots, a rucksack, and a Norfolk jacket. And from these the local security authorities had little difficulty in identifying the German 'tourist', who hiked around the strategic points of these islands before the war.

And he had four hours of a start.

When, in response to one of our own Lieutenant's more authoritative pep talks (with him waving his automatic pistol to emphasise his points), we sulked off to double the guards round the perimeter, the road between Garrabost and Bayble was congested with official-looking motor cars. While we crouched in terror behind what cover we could find (knowing what rotten shots our comrades were, and having just as little faith in the Home Guard), the alarm had run south into Harris, and the whole island was on the alert.

But the heather had hidden the stranger, without a trace.

While the Army and the Home Guard had taken over, the RAF was able to add its own findings, fortified with ample technical jargon. I had it myself over the tied line, from an RDF operator at Rodel Park, to the south of the island, that he had picked up on his set the trace of an unidentified object on the water, lying just off-shore.

This was confirmation that our spy had been landed from a submarine.

The children now spoke with none but the most senior officers, but made no more additions to their story than that the stranger seemed to have folded maps sticking out of his jacket pocket. The more closely they were questioned, the more tongue-tied they became, and at last answered questions with nothing but terrified weeping.

At this weary point, a police inspector from Stornoway, uninvited, took a run out to Bayble, more out of curiosity than from any desire to interfere in a ticklish military operation. But he was not refused when he asked modestly if he might be allowed to sit in on the latest interview with Sondag and Donaldina.

The familiar blue uniform held less terror for the children than the khaki of the security officers. This time they forgot to weep, and even showed a disposition to answer questions when the inspector asked if he might have a word with them in the Gaelic.

The postmaster later gave me a translation of this coversation.

'What did you do when you went for the cow?'

'We gathered flowers and played a game.'

'It was hard to find the cow?'

'Yes, she had strayed away towards Shader.'

'And you forgot about her for a while?'

'Yes.'

'And when you remembered again it was late?'

'Yes.'

'And then you were afraid that your mamma would be wild and give you a slap?'

'Yes.'

'So you made up the story about the stranger?'

'Yes.'

'And the boots and the haversack?'

'We saw them in a picture book.'

And, as Uncle George was not too blate to point out when we related this to him, if it's the Truth you are looking for, the only sure way to seek it is in the Gaelic.

———— * ————

It is a pity that I must leave this linguistic subject on a note of pessimism, but there is no doubt about the insidious and corrupting intrusion of domestic English upon the pure undefiled stream of the Gaelic. Even among its native speakers. And here I have the evidence of my own ears from a visit to a Hebridean games; when the light hammer was hurled off its intended course and landed on the foot of a little Highland boy among the spectators. Upon being struck by this fearsome projectile, he was heard to cry in despair, 'Tha me buggered, mamma.'

CHAPTER ELEVEN

WALKING WITH GREAT MEN

W<small>HEN</small>I was about twelve, and Hume Brown had brought us up to
the Reformation, a teacher asked my class, 'Who was John Calvin?' I
replied that he was a Free Church minister at present in the mission
field in Peru, that his full name was John Calvin Mackay, and that he
had just had enormous adventures in the Andes along with a medical
missionary called Kenny Mackay, who was another Highlander but no
relative. I was a little put out that the teacher should have heard of him
too, because I always regarded my connections with the Free Church,
and with the resolute people who passed through the Fearn manse, as
something exclusive, as a distinction that removed me a little from
the suburban Moderates in Bearsden, who sang hymns and sat down
to pray.

I was restored to learn that we were talking of two different people,
one of them an obscure Frenchman in whom I took no further
interest.

Before I was very old I considered myself a good judge of a minister,
not from what I heard him saying in the pulpit, because that was
always beyond my understanding, but from the way he behaved in the
study, and from the blessing he asked in the diningroom. I was
influenced too, perhaps, by the asides which I overheard behind the
scenes from Aunt Maggie, who was shrewd and had a talent that
amounted to virtuosity for making a brief, dry character sketch. Uncle
George was more circumspect and general, given to pointing the

116

excellence of those he considered great, and no more than hinting that there might be some with whom it would be uncharitable to make the comparison.

Each in their own way, Uncle George and Aunt Maggie led me to the same conclusions. Uncle George did it by bringing me up on *The Days of the Fathers in Ross-shire*, and showing me such giants as Dr Munro of Ferintosh, and that great and fiery Dr Kidd of Aberdeen who hurled the Book at a man in a red waistcoat, sleeping in his pew, crying: 'You rid-breisted sinner. If ye'll no' hear the word of God, ye'll feel it.'

He liked to see in his contemporaries that stamp of authority that joined the fear of the minister along with the fear of the Lord as the beginning of wisdom. It did his own morale good to see a back-slider taking to the fields on the approach of the manse phaeton. And he was as fly as any stalker at waylaying the sinner.

He enjoyed, as he would fain have had himself, the reputed omniscience of the Caithness catechiser who, on his way to visit a cottage, was seen from the distance by one Adam Sinclair, whose conscience was not fit for interrogation. Sinclair fled to warn the household, and on the way tripped and plunged into the dung heap. Filthy and unpresentable he hid below the bed. When the catechiser came in the house his first question was, 'Where did Adam fall?' And the goodwife said, 'Ye can come oot, Adam. There is nothing hid from the eyes of the righteous.'

Uncle George had his own congregation well in hand. We came one day unexpectedly among the farm servants' cottages at Balmuchy and a young ploughman was cornered before he could flee. He had not been at the church for four Sabbaths and, in the desperate need of an immediate excuse, he said that he had been ashamed to come for he was without decent boots. Uncle George bought him a pair that same afternoon in Balintore, and when he handed them over said, 'Now stay away at your peril.' His own peril was almost as grave when he had to try to explain the transaction to Aunt Maggie when we got home.

He watched with distrust the growth of a subtler psychological approach to the encouragement of good attendance, and regretted it as much as he did the increasing use of the dog-collar.

There were no dog-collars among the photographs that hung on the study wall. These were his friends, his companions in early secessions, and the men he venerated. There was a retouched portrait of Munro of Ferintosh in a heavy wood frame, to whom he would point when he thought I was needing an example. John Macdonald, the Apostle of the North, was there, too, good Caithness man that he was, and one that in his day must have known the Berriedale Brae better even than Uncle George.

Principal M'Culloch, whom I just remember as an austere and aged man with a thin face and flowing long white sidewhiskers, had the place above the mantelpiece, which he held until he was moved over above the desk to make way for the much larger portrait of Dr John Stuart Holden of St Paul's, Portman Square, London, whom Uncle George had met at the Keswick Convention and who was the only man who could ever induce him to listen to a hymn. The Low Church Episcopalian vicar and the Free Church minister were close friends for ten years. Uncle George valued him above all the Moderates in Scotland. Dr Stuart Holden came up from London once to preach from Uncle George's pulpit, and said of him then: 'He puts first things first; and as for the other things, he has no place for them at all.'

The other photographs I remember, apart from one of himself in his Moderator's robes, were of the two companions with whom, in 1905, he attempted, in vain, to heal the breach between the Free Presbyterians and the Free Church. These were Professor John MacLeod and Dr Alexander Stewart, Edinburgh. With them Uncle George left the Free Presbyterians, and lost a certain amount of the respect of my grandmother, who was relentless on election, and kept the 'tent' in one of the outhouses for use in the open-air services which she arranged from time to time as an opposition to the United Free Church across the road at Westerdale.

In my childhood at the manse the amiable practice of tipping children was still observed, and I measured the success of a Communion in terms of florins and half-crowns. A closer check on this source of income might have been kept had Aunt Maggie realised that it placed me in the position of being able to afford to indulge my craving for cigarettes, which I could then buy from my friend the driver of the grocer's van and smoked either in the henhouse or in my bedroom lying on my back with my head in the grate and blowing the reek up the chimney.

The best tippers were not necessarily those visitors I held in the highest esteem. They had to thole their test-piece long before the time came for their departure. On their first evening, always a week-day, after supper and before the Books, when we were sitting talking in the study, I would say, 'Tell me a story;' and on the reaction to that request

I decided whether the minister was worthy or not. To qualify for our good opinion (for this was a catechism in which my brother and cousins joined in their day) the story did not need to be funny, so long as it did not have a moral. For instance, I never had anything but the highest regard for the Rev. Donald Smith of Kiltearn, who was very deaf, although for a period of more than ten years he responded always and only with what he called a riddle: 'A tall man and a short man were fighting. The tall man knocked the short man down, then the short man knocked the tall man down. Who beat? You don't know? The maid beat the carpet.'

It was this same Mr Smith who, when once asked if he had ever ridden in George Mackay's car, replied, 'Yes, and I never felt nearer Eternity in my life.'

There was another, a pious and successful business man, who was ever willing to tell a long story but it never failed to be pompous and full of object lessons in thrift and industry, and since I had asked for it I always had to listen to it, while Uncle George, with the nearest approach that he ever came to a wink, would slip off to the morning room and make up sections for his beehives. No cash reward could restore that devout visitor to my regard, and to this day I believe that he just did not like children.

When enduring an improving story I always felt uneasy and fearful of being classified with a contemporary of their own of whom my mother and uncles used to tell. He was a sly and unctuous child who knew how to get round his godly grandmother. Climbing upon her knee he would say, 'Tell me a story, Nanna,' and when she said, 'Yes, what will I tell you, Robert? he would look up into her eyes and say, 'Tell me aboot Goad, Nanna.'

He found this good impression valuable against the discovery of any hellishness that he had in prospect.

Apart from the ministers who came at Communion time there were the students who came as 'supply' during Uncle George's frequent absences. Most of these lacked the confidence that would allow them to relax, and tended to be more censorious than the ministers. To one like me who walked on what he considered equal terms with the great men of the Church, however, their obvious inexperience was such that there was no call to take their gravity seriously.

I used to walk with them to the evening service and make a point of bringing up some purely secular and frivolous subject. For this I would be sternly reproved, and treated to a lecture on suitable-things-to-speak-of-on-the-Sabbath. I would hear it out meekly, then say, 'I am sorry, but I thought it was all right because that was what Uncle George and I were speaking about last Sabbath.'

The students were fairly frequent visitors, and I believed I could recognise the ones that would turn out to be good. But perhaps merit, like beauty, lies in the eye of the beholder, and there are circumstances in which the judgment of the beholder may be suspect.

The lay preachers were even less sure of themselves than the students. The responsibility of their entertainment lay often with myself alone, particularly when one of the more inviting Communions had taken Aunt Maggie away along with Uncle George. The problem of maintaining conversation lasted through Saturday afternoon, Sunday, and breakfast on Monday morning.

There were ministers who would admit to having read *Westward Ho!* Lay-preachers seemed to read only the Monthly Record. I had one difficult afternoon when our conversation had been a discussion on the praise with a close consideration of the Psalm tunes. We had soon stated all our preferences and had compared notes on the sol-fa in the divided Psalm book. The subject appeared to be exhausted, and it was still an hour until tea time. In order to keep it going I asked, 'What do you think of the Negro Spirituals?'

I never saw a man so shocked. 'You, in a manse,' he cried, 'ask me that? What would your uncle say?'

I said I did not see any harm in them and did not think Uncle George would either so long as we did not ask Johnny Urquhart to try precenting them. He remained horrified, so I asked if he knew anything about them. He said no, thank God, but he had once heard a profane man singing one, and it had a verse that began 'Young folks, old folks' and went on to say that it would tell you Bible stories that you'd never heard before.

I never had much opportunity for confirming the popular impression that ministers' sons are wilder than the limbs of the laity. The only one of them with whom I had an acquaintance stopped for a long week-end once at Fearn. He was two years older than I and had just left school, and he was on the way to the university, with his first soft hat. I hid the hat and he beat me up, which was a good sign.

We sat up all one night in order to go down to the village at dawn to see the fishing boats come in, and we chewed quids of Uncle George's bogey roll tobacco to keep us awake, which was promising and sickening. Before we left we went to the byre and milked the cow for our early breakfast, and we arrived back at the manse in mid-forenoon at the same time as the vet, who had been sent for to find out why she had gone dry, which was excellent.

In the evening we went fishing in a boat on Loch Eye along with one or two of the farm loons from Rhynie, and we lost every hook we had and got no fish. Throughout that expedition our visitor sat in the stern of the boat and never said a word. But when we got ashore and were on our way together back to the manse, he said, 'Were you not afraid?'

I said no, and he said, 'But did you not hear those boys? Every time they lost a hook they said swearwords, and I was sure the boat would sink below us before we got back to the shore.'

He has been a minister, like his father, these many years.

CHAPTER TWELVE

TRAVELLING OCCASIONS

Uncle George was, in his own way, a courageous and experienced horseman, as was only to be expected in a man who on occasion had attempted to ride Henderson's horses. These were probably the only hacks that ever had the distinction of a pulpit rebuke. Nor was his the courage of ignorance, and he would not have you think so, for every time he told a story of one of his adventurous journeys to a Communion or a funeral or a wedding, he would say: 'And mind you I knew I was putting my hand on my life.'

He had not the horseman's figure or the seat of a Cunninghame-Graham, for he ran more to breadth than to elegance, and he would as soon have worn a dog-collar as breeches. Except that he wore a tile hat on the Sabbath and a black felt on week-days, his outdoor costume remained the same from the day he was ordained until the day he died. He wore black or a very dark grey, and the vest buttoned right up to the neck, where it ended in a small cut-out, about an inch deep and two wide, to show his linen, which consisted of a 'Shakespeare' collar and a white tie. These collars were hard to come by, for I have been with Aunt Maggie when she went, one after the other, to all the important haberdashers in Glasgow, asking with a certain mim pride for Shakespeare collars and receiving everywhere the same blank stare.

'You know' — she would say — 'for Free Church ministers': and such was her esteem for Uncle George and his prejudices that she flounced out in fine indignation every time she was offered a dog-collar.

You don't see many Shakespeare collars now. They are flat and narrow, with a wide opening and long peaks — indeed, a little 'Edwardian'. I went to the Free Church Assembly in more recent years, and when I found but one, and it surmounting a neat light grey suit, I saw with sorrow that we had fallen upon new days in which even Moderates might be flattered with respect. And when that same Assembly accepted a motion deploring the popular use of the epithet 'Wee Free', my disillusion was confirmed. Uncle George revelled in being a Wee Free. It made him feel tough and invincible — the heir to great men who fought against odds from the lower courts to the House of Lords, and won. He never saw 'Wee' as any belittling of his spirit or the breadth of his mind.

He also wore made-up ties. They were fashioned by Aunt Maggie out of white linen tape. He had fine linen cuffs for Sunday and celluloid ones for work about the house and the glebe. They were not anchored and were awkward, but Aunt Maggie believed in keeping up appearances, even if it meant that, when he weeded the walk or mucked the byre too heartily, he had to stop every few minutes to retrieve his right cuff from where it revolved round the bottom end of the handle of the hoe or the graip.

Uncle George, whose vanities lay in other directions, was never jealous of his physical dignity. If he found a strange hat on the hall stand, and thought when he tried it on — as he always did — that he looked funny in it, he paraded through the house until every resident member of the family had shared the joke.

His hair, which was thinning on top even when I first knew him, was well tufted and thick above the ears. When he fell asleep in his chair, as he usually did after the mid-morning smoke, I used to twist the tufts into horns, which, since I normally had jammy fingers, stuck out firmly and well from his brows. He delighted in those horns, for often he would wear them all day, in defiance of Aunt Maggie, who felt that, however informal he might be in the family circle, it hardly did for a Free Church minister to be impersonating Satan when refined farmers came to tea, and humble members of the congregation came for advice, or a 'character'.

This indifference to dignity was equally pronounced when duty called. He well knew what he looked like on horseback. Once in a winter of his early days at Stornoway he was trysted to preach at Ness

(I think it was), and set out in the early morning to cross the island by gig. He had hardly left the shelter of the town street when he ran into snow drifts, which completely blocked the road and he had to turn back. This was too easy an admission of defeat, and when he returned to Henderson's he said, 'We'll ride.' And he was off again, with a stable boy for esquire. But the boy lost heart when his horse sat down, and he turned and went home. Uncle George, with his trousers tucked into his socks and his cuffs in his pocket, carried on and made a hole, head-first, into every snowdrift for the next half-mile. He used to say that he would have persevered if it had not been for the horse which, after it had been over the head in a ditch, turned its face to Stornoway and refused to try another step in the direction of the Butt of Lewis. He led it back, for, once the responsibility for the retreat was plainly put on the horse, he found himself ready to admit that he no longer had the strength to pull himself again into the saddle.

He got to Ness, though. Limping back to the manse he went past the water front and saw a fishing coble heading out of the harbour. One of his congregation was at the helm. He hailed it, and the fisherman, who had merely intended to push his nose out for a closer look at the gurly sea, found himself beating up the east coast of the Eye Peninsula with a minister for passenger. How he was feeling you may know from the fact that even on a fair day a Lewis fisherman would go home and shut the door if, on his way down to the boat, he met a minister. When they came to Ness the minister was baling. He had a fisherman's oily on him, but his tile hat was still on his head. It was by that that the congregation had known him when they sighted the boat labouring in the sea, and, since they were all on the jetty to meet him, he had his service there and then. He was so delighted with the sensation of his arrival that he forgot to put on his cuffs. 'They were awful limp, anyway,' he said.

The sea, in fact, held few terrors for him. He knew the Minch almost as well as he knew the captain of the Sheila, who had carried him on more voyages than he could put a number on between Stornoway and Kyle. Sometimes he was even allowed to take the helm. Coming back from the mainland, he once became involved in a doctrinal dispute with a number of Moderate ministers who were on their way to Lewis. That was as good a way as any of fighting the tedium of the long railway journey by Achnasheen and Achnashellach to Kyle, and of the weary voyage up past Skye and on to the Long Island. Uncle George always claimed that he had the better of them that day; he never said in so many words, however, that it was in the verbal battle that he prevailed.

It must have been something dogmatic that sent him at last to cool off on the bridge, and it was while passing the time of day there with the captain that he looked forward and saw his half-brethren of the Auld Kirk standing together near the bows.

'Maybe I might take the wheel now?' he asked the captain, who saw no objection.

'Then,' he would say to whoever of us was getting the story, 'I waited until I saw a fine big curly one, and I put her nose right into it. And before I rightly had time to bring her back, those Moderates, with the spray still shining on their whiskers, were up the ladder roaring, "Take the wheel away from that madman, Captain. He'll have us all drowned and he doesn't care."'

One way or another, he felt he had taught them to argue with a Wee Free.

I was better acquaint, however, with Uncle George the horseman than with Uncle George the sailor. At Fearn, until the motor came to satisfy his taste for danger, he bowled through his parish in a lean black phaeton, and he liked to have it drawn by a lively high-stepper. His noble taste in horseflesh let him down, for, when he came back with Aunt Maggie from a visit to the Black Isle in the spring of 1915, he found that the stable-boy and the horse had gone off together to enlist. He missed that horse, a big black charger that kicked and had a lot of white in his eye, and always kept his ears laid back.

Then he got Dotty, a compact dapple grey of about 13.5 hands, and for the next few years he could be met almost any afternoon on any of the roads in the triangle marked by Tain, Nigg and Portmahomack, the phaeton on the verge, and the horse unyoked, and himself holding on the end of the reins and whipping her round him like a ringmaster training Liberties. Dotty was a refuser.

She was a natural refuser, but she went well enough after a thrashing. But Uncle George never understood why the lesson never lasted more than a few days. The fault lay with Aunt Maggie, who was not tender hearted but was afraid of the horse. She tried to do by persuasion what Uncle George did with the whip, and when she went driving alone she always carried on the floor of the phaeton a basket of small green apples. They were hard little apples, the only fruit that the manse trees produced, and Dotty, alone among us, was partial to them.

Aunt Maggie hated to make a spectacle of herself, and suffered dreadful embarrassment when the horse would suddenly stop in the middle of the road and go no farther. Clicking and clucking was never of any use, and if you used the whip from the back seat of the phaeton Dotty just started backing until she had the carriage in the ditch. Aunt Maggie had no stomach for the spectacular thrashing. She got down with an apple in each hand, and offered them to the mare, saying, 'Dotty, Dotty. Clever, now.' And then Dotty became quite biddable and would answer the reins until she had lost the taste of the apples. Then she would stop and wait to be fed again.

At eleven years old I was confident of my ability to master Dotty. But I was not allowed to demonstrate it. I got my chance, however, once when Aunt Maggie and Uncle George had been away for the week-end and were expected home on the evening train at Fearn Station, four miles away from the manse. I would take out the horse and phaeton and go and meet them. The young woman teacher from Balmuchy School who was living with us at the time and was nominally in charge, forbade it. When I defied her she washed her hands of the affair, shutting herself up in her room, and I had to catch and harness the horse without her assistance, on which I had counted. I managed it, though, even if I left off the breeching, to which Dotty was sensitive, and did not manage to draw the girth as tight as it should have been.

I cracked the whip and yodelled as we came spanking past the manse and through the trees until we were pulled up by the double iron gate to the driveway. Here again I had been expecting assistance, but the windows behind me remained blind. I dropped the reins and got down and swung the gates open with a slam right under Dotty's nose. She took fright and reared. The saddle with the slack girth, and without the breeching to tether it, slipped forward; the traces twisted, the trams tripped the horse, and she came down on her foreknees. The teacher and the servant lassie then came out from where they had been hiding behind a curtain, and we manhandled the phaeton back into the coach-house. The remaining time until the arrival of the family I spent in the stable, swabbing the blood from Dotty's knees and rubbing them with burnt cork and butter, as much to hide the wounds as to heal them.

That was another time Uncle George got out the ebony stick.

—— * ——

126

In the year 1924 the machine age overtook my Uncle George and he bought a motor car. About the same time he stopped wearing the tile hat, and took to the soft black wideawake felt, saving the silk for the Sabbath, and for the short walk to and from the car and the vestry at funerals and weddings. From then on the old, shaped, leather hat-box with the strap round it became one of the permanent obstacles among the feet of passengers on the back seat. The other was a large square kerbstone, weighing about half-a-hundredweight, introduced by Aunt Maggie, always practical, who was afraid that Uncle George would stall the engine while trying to change down on a steep hill.

The hat-box also went with him on his train journeys when he came south to the Assembly and to the communions at which he was constantly assisting up and down the Highland Line. He was very absentminded about it, as he was about many things, but he was well known to the railway company in the days when the trains were a more personal service than they are now. His tile hat was familiar on railway carriage racks from Wick to Inverness, and from Dingwall to Kyle, and from Inverness to Perth or Aberdeen.

He got off once at Aviemore leaving the hat, as usual, behind him. It carried on to Glasgow. A week later the carrier brought it from the station to the manse. There was a Buchanan Street Station label on it with the printed instruction 'Try Mackay, Fearn'.

At Perth Station porters when they looked into an empty compartment and saw a tile hat on the rack used to pass round the word that Reverend George was on his travels again. Sometimes the porter at Bonar Bridge, seeing him deep in conversation with a fellow-passenger in the north-bound train, would interrupt to tell him that he had gone four stops beyond his home station.

This gift of detachment lent an exciting quality to his motoring. He held the steering wheel as casually as he had been accustomed to hold the reins, and he expected from his car the same road sense he had always found in his horses that, once guided into the right direction, knew where to go and went there, leaving him free to follow his thoughts into the perorations which he loved to polish.

He first took the ditch near Kildary three weeks after he got the car, while on his way, alone, to an Education Authority meeting in Dingwall. For that he blamed a reactionary fellow-member whom he had intended to trounce that afternoon. He was rehearsing his remarks and had forgotten about driving.

'When I came to "and lastly, Mr Chairman," I stamped my foot on the floor and beat the table with my right hand, but my foot was on the accelerator and my hand was on the wheel,' he explained some hours later when Aunt Maggie was picking thorns out of his face with tweezers and rubbing the cuts with iodine.

When a ploughman from Balnagown who had seen the swerve pulled him out of the wild rose bush in which he had landed head first, he was saying, 'I move the previous question.'

From that time he travelled always with a co-pilot. There was no back-seat driving. Aunt Maggie sat beside him. She kept his mind on the road and gave fair warning of corners, calling sharply, 'The horn, Cheorge, the horn.'

He was inclined, however, to zig-zag a little when suddenly faced with the additional movement of taking one hand from the wheel and fumbling for the bulb which stuck out from below the right-hand side of the dashboard. This did not matter much on the roads between Tain in the north and Invergordon in the south, where motorists and cart drivers knew to be on the look-out for him.

But we had ambitions of travelling farther afield, and in preparation for a journey to Caithness Aunt Maggie wrote a letter to Messrs Macrae and Dick in Dingwall, who sent her by return of post the biggest bulb horn they had in stock. She kept it in the pocket of the near-side door along with her knitting, and on the road she carried it clasped firmly between her knees.

'You attend to the driving, Cheorge,' she said at the approach to every bend and on the most distant sight of any oncoming traffic, 'and

I'll see to the horn.' And she did, with such sustained aggressiveness that at one time or another she must have scared every horse in Easter Ross. The cows used to come down from the fields to watch us passing with their heads stuck over the hedges, and the young bulls used to pace us, bellowing, with their tails straight up in the air.

It was many years before Aunt Maggie picked up any of the technical and mechanical jargon of motoring, and, even then, her advice for the treatment of any engine failure was the same — 'Wash out the carbooraytor.' What she said to all passengers before setting out on an excursion was, 'Now remember, if we are going up a hill and the motor suddenly stops, you jump out, clever, and put that stone under the back wheel.'

The stone was still there two cars later, for she never learned to trust either motor cars or Uncle George as driver.

He was forbidden to use hand signals. Turns to the left Aunt Maggie indicated herself by leaning over her own door and waving. Turns to the right were the responsibility of any passenger who happened to be in the back seat. This team work became a tradition that was continued even into the later saloon car that had red, amber, and green traffic indicators on each side.

What Uncle George really wanted was a long, low, open sports car with a noisy exhaust and a horn that sounded three savage notes. You could see that when he pulled his hat down over his brow and, with a reckless look and a canny corner of his eye on Aunt Maggie, would push the old Citroen up to thirty miles an hour.

But the horn between Aunt Maggie's knees was used to warn Uncle George as well as other road users. Two honks and he knew he was found out, and the car settled back into an easy hand-canter. This was hard discipline on a man who, until he reached the age of 56, had been namely for the high-steppers that he drove in his phaeton.

It also meant that he never got a good run at a hill, so that the stone was often under the back wheel. We did not mind this so much on our own territory, but we felt it made us conspicuous on our longer journeys. Special precautions were taken for the crossing of the Ord into Caithness and on the Berriedale Brae. Climbing over the Ord we in the back seat had to keep the doors open to be ready to jump out.

But when we came to the top of the descent into Langwell we had to get down, with the stone in our arms, and walk near the front of the car lest Uncle George missed first gear or the brakes failed. On the equally steep rise up the other side we stood on the running boards, usually one cousin on each flank, while Aunt Maggie directed the ascent from her control office on the front seat.

If we stuck, as we often did, on the hairpin bend halfway up — those were the days, before it had been straightened out, when you looked over the poor retaining wall apparently right into the sea 200 ft below — the car was not restarted, and we waited for a farm horse to come and tow us over the hump and on to the level, or for a more experienced driver to abandon his own car and take over from Uncle George.

To the last Aunt Maggie had a prim and dignified approach to motoring. In the early days of the tourer she tied her hat down with a veil. This was necessary because after the first ditching she thought we would be safer without the side curtains, and they were stacked, never to be used again, in the corner of the old coachhouse which the car shared with the hens after the old phaeton had been taken to the barn which it was no longer necessary to fill with hay.

She, a redoubtable quarter-master, had always negotiated for the fodder for the horse. Mechanised, she naturally took the responsibility for refuelling the car. She was to be seen at her best at a filling station, when, after a measuring glance at the gauge, she would summon the attendant and say, 'We will have three gallons of petroleum, if you please?'

She always seemed sorry that the transaction was completed without giving her a chance of haggling a little before she struck her bargain.

CHAPTER THIRTEEN

THE MACAPHEE SUB-CULTURE

IN her exchanges and transactions with the tinkers, on
her home ground, Aunt Maggie tended to come off second best.
Her intentions were always of the most sensibly Christian, and
her concern for their welfare was as sincere as it might seem to
be manorial. And she suffered, though she bore it with resignation,
a certain loss of countenance when her interlocutors made no
concessions to the precise seemliness of her own speech.

Her interest in the travelling folk, with whom she had been familiar
all her life on the homestead doorstep, was quite personal, for she
knew many of them by name and background, and was often aware of
their particular misfortunes, as when she heard that one regular
whiner at the kitchen door had fallen ill.

Recognising a jet-haired, black-eyed daughter as she passed before
the house, walking at the tail of the spring-cart, Aunt Maggie stopped
her, to say, 'Now tell me. How is your father?'

'He's a bittie better the day,' came the instant reply. 'He's fartin'.'

It may not have been my aunt's idea of an ideal diagnosis; but there
is no doubt it had its validity.

Uncle James, on the other hand, met the tinkers, as it were, on their
own ground and in their own idiom. After all he had a long record of
dealing with them, usually in the matter of horse-coping, where he
sometimes won, but generally lost. Horses bought from the tinkers
frequently turned out to be spavined, or refusers. But he had his little

victories, as on the day — and I was there — when a caravan of Macaphees was halted on the road just before the house. It was halted against the will of the driver of the leading cart, and just because the horse refused to budge.

The tinker used all the persuasions in his repertory, from cajoling to whipping, and at last in despair gathered a bundle of straw and set it alight under the horse's belly. But all the beast did was to take three paces forward and stop again, leaving the cart in danger of going up in flames.

Standing in the kitchen door Uncle James watched the scene with infinite content and complacency, intervening at last to say, 'Would you like me to help?'

'If ye can,' condescended the Macaphee.

Whereupon Uncle James returned into the kitchen where a dozen potatoes in their jackets were roasting on the earth. Picking up the hottest of these, and tossing it from hand to hand, he went out into the road and deftly inserted it under the horse's tail, which instinctively clamped down. The horse and cart went off like a bullet, and as they disappeared over the crest of the hill Uncle James turned and said smugly, 'Well, what do you think now?'

'I think now,' replied the Macaphee, 'that ye should jist go back intil the hoose and get anither ane tae pit in my erse so that I can catch him.'

—— * ——

The Caithness tinkers, who are not to be confused with Romanies or gypsies, were, and no doubt still are, Williamsons, Macaphees — and, not irrelevantly, Sinclairs. As far back as memory goes they have been their own intimate and distinctive part of the community with whom they worked out a generally amiable and tolerant *modus vivendi*. I do not pretend to know how they do nowadays except that they are thoroughly motorised.

But they used to have their own special integration, a peculiar sort of acceptable Caithness caste system; so that during the First World War, when conscription gathered everyone in its net, the relationship continued, and the crofter private soldiers of the Seaforth Highlanders had their own informal batmen in the mud of Flanders. Uncle James was one of them, and I used to hear him reminiscing at the dykeside with the Williamson whom he had informally employed to winkle out the lice in the seams of his shirt and the pleats of his kilt.

132

The relationship, indeed, might have been just a little closer than the settled population of those parts would readily admit. I am remembering — again through the voice of my mother — a cousin of my grandfather's, who was in a good way of business in Halkirk, an honest man, who had brought up his family to have a properly good conceit of themselves. With his young son, he was one day visiting at Westerdale, and while they were standing by the garden gate a handsome carriage passed carrying a clutch of apparently aristocratic fishing tenants, bound for the Loch More Lodge.

'Pa,' said the boy hopefully, watching them disappear in a flurry of dust, 'Are we gentry?'

'No, my son,' replied our kinsman. 'Not gentry, but just a little better than the commonalty of the people.'

This however was a status which was somewhat shaken the same day when he was accosted familiarly by a tinker — also of the name of Sinclair, and clearly an instinctive phrenologist — who claimed a family relationship, saying, 'Ye see. Yur back o' heid same as my back o' heid.'

—— * ——

There was no lock on the back door that opened directly into the kitchen, just a latch. It was not a lack that caused any anxiety. On the contrary.

The last duty at night was to draw aside two of the iron slats on the hearth, and with the tongs to take the burning peats and plunge them into the fine ash in the pit. There they remained until morning when, picked out and re-set on the grid, it took only a blow from the bellows to set them into a glow and a flame again, and ready to take the porridge pot.

I can remember, more than once, Granny or one of the aunts coming into the kitchen first thing in the morning, looking at the hearth and saying matter-of-factly, 'I see the tinkers were in last night.'

Any benighted wayfarer, and at that time and in that place this simply meant the travelling folk, was welcome to lift the latch, make up the fire, and take their rest without disturbing the family. And be on their way before dawn, after 'resting' the fire again. There was an unmentioned and honourable understanding about this. On the road and in the daylight it was taken for granted that the Macaphees and their kind operated on the principle of finders-keepers. But they were meticulous about the sanctity of the loose latch and the implied hospitality of the open door at night. When they came in out of the blast into a kitchen furnished with pickings of food and gear, all they took was the warmth of the fire. The understanding was tacit, and I would rather not know whether it is still so.

—— * ——

I have mentioned the Liberal political tradition of Caithness which was (apparently finally) broken soon after the last war when to his great surprise and visible chagrin, the late Sir Archibald Sinclair (not yet Lord Thurso) was defeated in a General Election. The victor, if my memory serves, was a Tory character called Gander Dower.

Thereafter the laird's visits to his Caithness estates were private, and reclusively informal. In fact, when he came north in the summer he stayed quietly in a shooting lodge, far into the hill and well off the beaten track. The only immediate problem that this presented was the availability of domestic help. This, however, for the modest requirements of the occasion, was adequately met by the employment of a mature tinker couple. And the arrangement, with its minimal demands, worked perfectly until the arrival in Thurso of some distinguished Londoners, whom it was thought proper to invite to the lodge for afternoon tea.

I have only the local circumstantial report for the denouement; but I have always had implicit faith in the Caithness grapevine.

For the occasion a silver tea-set was produced, and the staff was carefully briefed; principally to have everything ready and waiting when the drawing room bell rang.

There was, however, a delay; the conversation had lapsed a little, and the company was therefore attentive when the doors were thrust open, and the temporary major-domo, tidied up, and wearing a collar

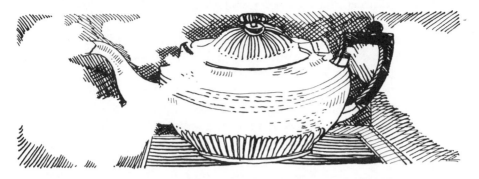

and tie, entered (without the tea-trolley) to announce: 'There'll be nae tea, yir leddyship. The airse is oot o' the teapot.'

The briefing had been incomplete. It had reckoned without the established Macaphee method of infusing tea, which involved placing the vessel on the red hot hob of the stove.

—— * ——

For a quarter of a century at least, politics was no problem in the North-east; and particularly in Ross and Cromarty where, when the occasion regularly arose, the folk just automatically voted for Sir Ian Macpherson, Baronet, their Liberal, who was more or less a native son. And a distinguished one at that, having been Under-Secretary for War, Chief Secretary for Ireland, Minister of Pensions; with the slightly earlier distinction of having been, at once, the youngest Cabinet Minister, the youngest Privy Councillor, and the youngest King's Counsel. He was also, which was no local disadvantage, the Chief of the Gaelic Society of London and a Freeman of Dingwall.

In these circumstances Uncle George had no occasion to be overtly political in his transactions with his flock. But in the wild January of 1936, a season of snowbound roads and blizzards, Sir Ian Macpherson had the reward of his eminence and was elevated to the peerage as Baron Strathcarron of Banchor, County Inverness. This coincided with the Coalition Ministry of Stanley Baldwin, and sparked off a curious by-election, not the least element of which was its revelation of a devious, Jesuitical facet to the character of my simon-pure uncle.

The campaign was as curious as it was impolite in that of the four candidates only one carried a plain label. He was the late Hector McNeil, who was Labour. Malcolm MacDonald, the son of the former Prime Minister, was National Labour and National. Dr Russell Thomas was Independent Liberal, and Randolph Churchill was Independent Unionist.

For the first time Uncle George manifestly showed his colours, which turned out to be a shade of pink, which the family felt did not suit him, particularly when they heard of the manner in which he had been canvassing his flock. On pain of what divine retribution I would rather not speculate, but he went round the fishing villages and the farm cottages, ostensibly in his role as shepherd, but taking the occasion to dare his people to vote for any other than Malcolm MacDonald. Where there were Socialist 'don't-knows', he persuaded them, with the infallibility of his cloth, that the other Labour man was not really of the true faith. This was very effective canvassing, for he would be alternating his political exhortation with the expected little sessions of family prayer. I did not hear that he had done any proselytising around the wealthier farm houses — where indeed he was seldom asked to pray, but just invited to put up a word of grace over the tea-table.

When taxed with his politicking at home he was unrepentant, and, of course was smug and took a good deal of personal credit for it when Malcolm MacDonald won.

It must be conceded however, that Uncle George was not the only minister who imposed a powerful influence on that by-election, in which, by his ignorance of whom he was dealing with, Randolph Churchill turned out to be the tainted wether of that odd flock of candidates. Flown with insolence and pride he had come north to lecture the hinds, and to denounce the lack of independence among Scottish Unionists who had just voted Ramsay MacDonald into the vacant Scottish Universities seat.

Now in his retirement, the Very Rev. Dr Lauchlan MacLean Watt, one of the most formidable giants of the Auld Kirk, had withdrawn to Wester Ross, where he was the most venerated member of the community. At a meeting at Loch Carron, when Randolph delivered himself intemperately upon the subject of Ramsay MacDonald and his University seat, Dr MacLean Watt interrupted with a cry of 'Shame'. The candidate, looking down on his audience saw only an aged, and probably ignorant Highland person, to whom he replied curtly and contemptuously. And in a moment the atmosphere in the hall was as tempestuous and angry as the weather outside. When the first exchange did not go his way Randolph got rude; and Ramsay MacDonald was soon forgotten when Dr MacLean Watt, an old campaigner in Presbytery and Assembly disputes and debates, enlarged his attack with supplementary questions about the price of barley, to which the young Churchill, not surprisingly, could not give the answers. In the end, taking the defeated's refuge, he shouted that he would not be hectored or bullied by some contumacious old man in a country school hall.

For Randolph Churchill the Ross-and-Cromarty by-election was just about as humiliating as that earlier, famous, election at Dundee had been for his father, when Winston was defeated, not by a conventional opposition politico, but by one Danny Scrimgeour, a teetotal whisky-abolitionist candidate.

Whether Uncle George, were he alive to-day, would have been a supporter of the Liberal/SDP Alliance, must remain in doubt. All I can say is that he was acquainted, and had a charitable empathy with the great-grand aunt of the present member for the constituency of Caithness and Sutherland. She came from Rogart, where the family was engaged in the licensed trade; and on lamb-sale evenings she was from time to time to be seen on her knees in a quiet corner of the railway station at Lairg. The agreed explanation to any strangers who might draw her posture to the attention of the porter or the station-master, was that she was praying, as the spirit moved her, in the time-honoured manner of the itinerant Good Men of the North.

While Randolph Churchill experienced the rougher side of the MacLean Watt tongue, it is only due to his memory to recall that MacLean Watt was equally quick with the soft answer when he had a worthier interlocutor. When he was a chaplain during the First World War, he conducted a burial service over several men in his sector of the line. After the service, a Roman Catholic chaplain turned up and protested that Dr MacLean Watt had buried one of his flock. The Presbyterian peacemaker patted his priestly colleague on the shoulder, with the reassurance: 'Never mind. Christ will have sorted them out by now.'

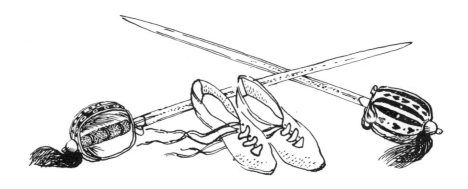

CHAPTER FOURTEEN

FUN AND GAMES

Bᴀʟʟʀᴏᴏᴍ dancing, theatres, and cinemas were, naturally enough, anathema to Uncle George, along with such Papish vanities as Christmas parties and midnight masses. Here his Free Presbyterian source flowed strong in him. He was not averse, perhaps, to a Highland Fling or a Sword Dance, if high spirits inspired them; but contact dancing, even in such formal and remotely tactile formations as the Lancers, was a dangerous incitement to lust and looseness. The only concession he would make in this regard was that he would have no positive objection to a man and his wife coming together in the Waltz; though he could not for his life imagine why they should want to. As for the theatre, there were plenty of words in the Old Testament to describe actresses; while actors were just flawed fellows who could, and should, be better employed.

He had no time for no-vells of any sort, and that went for Scott and Dickens too. Fiction to him was just a pack of lies.

He was deeply suspicious of Hollywood as a latter-day Gomorrah, having heard wanton hints of the life-style of such celebrities as Theda Bara and Pola Negri. I do not know in what company he picked it up, but he knew the word 'vamp', and used it in much the same context as he would have referred to the Whore of Babylon. It was therefore an outstanding achievement when, after much persuasion, he allowed me to take him to see *Ben Hur* (the original film with Ramon Navarro in the lead) in the Picture House in Aberdeen. I expected a demonstration, but as it turned out, my only problem was to keep him in his seat and try to calm him down during the chariot race, in which Francis X. Bushman got his come-uppance. That was the only film he ever saw, and though it did not offend him, he chose to regard it as a single exception to the libidinous rule.

Uncle George's idea of the perfect enjoyment of leisure was a forenoon in the morning-room, beatified in the smoke of pipefuls of Warlock tobacco, making frames for the honeycombs from the prefabricated slat strips of light wood, dovetailed at the ends; which we then folded into square sections with a strip of dimpled wax sheet in the middle to give the bees a start at building their honeycomb. There were also bigger, flatter ones that we made for the lower, breeding, section of the hives.

This diversion to be rounded off with the excursion to the bottom of the garden, with his carbolic cloth trailing from his pocket, to check how industriously his bees were filling up the combs in the hive labelled 'Sustentation Fund' — that would be the one that was dedicated to 'the maintenance of the ministry', a subject that, in slightly different ways, was equally dear to the hearts of himself and of Aunt Maggie. Uncle George's concern was general; Aunt Maggie's particular and closer to home.

Indeed it was my apprenticeship in this constructive pastime that, in much later years, stood me in good stead when I was dragooned (with somewhat more complicated kits) into cutting out and building balsa-wood models of Spitfires and other World War II aircraft.

— * —

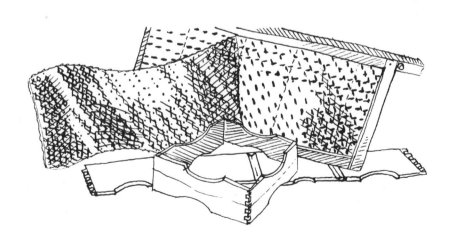

Uncle George had a sliding scale of anathema. His denunciation was graduated in descending order from the best of his execrations which he pronounced with great enjoyment on the Church of Rome to the tolerant disapproval with which he eventually regarded football pools. He had preached against the pools for a number of years before a member of the congregation won £100, and persuaded him that this was really a reward for skill, and that the penny points were as honest a way of making money as the buying of shares.

This was a clever line of argument, for Uncle George, under Aunt Maggie's guidance, took a deep and respectful interest in his small investments. When I came to the manse that year, some weeks after the windfall — I think it was the second horseman at Lochslin who had won the prize — I learned that while football pools might be said to entice the mind from higher things, they were not in themselves evil, nor indeed as blameworthy as the whist drives with which the Moderate at Fearn Abbey sought to win the favour of his congregation.

Uncle George's favourite travel book, indeed the only one I ever saw him read or heard him quote, was *Jacob Primmer in Rome*. It was authorised Sabbath reading, and because it contained an illustration by my father, who was otherwise a source of some sorrow since he was a journalist who wrote on Sundays, it was, a little grudgingly perhaps, counted to him for righteousness.

Toward all things but the papacy Uncle George discovered in himself as he grew older some slight capacity for compromise. While he made no direct concessions he could, when he chose, or when family affection demanded, avoid seeing what would offend him or call for his censure. Thus I know little of him as a visiting preacher in Glasgow.

He might arrive from the north and stay with us on Thursday and Friday night. But on Saturday afternoon he would leave us for a manse in town, ostensibly to be covenient to the church at which he was trysted for the Sabbath, and we would not see him again till Monday afternoon. This spared him the equal distress of riding in public transport on a Sunday and seeing one of his nearest relatives drawing cartoons or writing.

The Sunday papers were to him the work of the devil himself and fit only for those who, as he described them, gabbled their devotions in the morning and played football in the afternoon. His conscience asked him no questions when he read Monday's paper.

He had an unexampled command of the discreditable parts of the history of the Roman Catholic Church. He loved the Borgias for the wickedness that played into his hands, and he was as fluent on simony as he was, in other circumstances, on sanctification.

He was once taken for a priest on Dingwall Station and reckoned, with infectious relish, that he got in some first-rate subversive propaganda before he was found out. At the bottom of the garden the beehive next to the one marked 'Sustentation Fund' was labelled 'Foreign Missions'. To Uncle George foreign missions did not mean bringing Christianity to pagans in Africa; they meant the Free Church station at Lima, in Peru, where, so far as I understood him, the object was to convert Roman Catholics.

I learned about the Inquisition and the Iron Virgin from Jacob Primmer who, on these subjects, was as lusty as Buffalo Bill. The rest I had from overhearing Uncle George, whose best-told story was paraphrased from *Harry Lorrequer,* a no-vell by Charles Lever, which had been recommended to him early in his ministry as containing some good tales at the expense of the papacy. Only on the promise of such reward would he look at fiction. But when his guests were jovial and Rome was in derision he would admit his excursion into secular literature to tell of the Irish Dragoon, the stout Protestant, who was incensed at the frequency of the appearance of the parish priests at the regimental mess, where the food and wine were good, and of the reprisal that he took.

As officer of the day, he primed and instructed his sentries so that when late at night the clergy, well fed and rosily disguised in wine, set out for home they were challenged for the password. To four sentries, one after the other, and each deafer than the last, they had to roar, so that the whole delighted and anti-clerical camp might hear them, before they were allowed to pass, 'Bloody end to the Pope.'

This, he said, was rough soldier talk, but, in the circumstances, excusable.

There were in Uncle George's day no Roman Catholics in Lewis and Harris, and there were few and these self-conscious in Easter Ross. They were not an immediate threat but a distant menace to be deplored in general and anathematised on principle.

The hysteria of the recurring religious revivals in the Islands was a nearer problem, and if there was one person the Free Church minister disliked more than a priest it was a hymn-singing hot-gospeller. When one such passed through the Islands a minister might expect to see his congregation disturbed for years with catalepsies and trances.

Uncle George's preaching was minatory rather than ecstatic, and he did not take it as a compliment to his eloquence if a woman in the body of the church screamed 'Hallelujah' and, rolling her eyes back until only the whites showed, held her arms above her head so rigid that her companions could not pull them down. When that sort of thing happened he would try to ignore the interruption, but that frequently merely made the demonstration more extreme, and even he would lose the thread of his discourse.

I have seen the recollection of real fear on him when he spoke of such revivals, and of the meetings, continued in the black houses long into the night, where frenzy and peat smoke combined to give the service the quality of voodoo.

The almost-spent breath of such a revival once drifted eastward and stirred a faint inquiring interest in Fearn. The only active reaction it had was on the manse maid, who did not really know what it was all about but felt it her duty to her position to make a show of devotion. At a prayer meeting, where Uncle George was not preaching but giving a historical sketch of the Prophets, she suddenly stood up in her place and bellowed, 'I'm saved.'

She had a strong voice, and she was a heavy girl whom it took three of the congregation to carry out. Back in the manse Uncle George spoke to her in the study. She was a bit subdued the next day with a tendency to weep, but the day after that she was swearing again, and her own self.

Hymns Uncle George shunned in general because he understood that 'Lead Kindly Light' was written by John Henry Newman at the time when he was about to turn to Rome. He also thought they lacked the rugged character that jutted out of 'By Babel's Streams' when sung to 'Belmont'. And though, after a visit to the Keswick Convention late in his life, he brought home a Church Hymnary, just to look at, he would never concede that there was anything in it as good as 'I to the Hills' to 'French', and it never reached the church. That was as well, for the precentor was hard enough pressed to give a lead to 'Covenanters' or 'Stroudwater'. The Gaelic congregation were never in any danger. They put out the line, and to do that, you need a tune like 'Stornoway'.

It pleased him that the Moderates and the United Free Church led the praise with an organ. This gave him the opportunity, at times he was likely to be suitably overheard, to wonder aloud when they were going to have the fiddlers in, or maybe a man with the bagpipes. If it came to that he would be willing, he said, to lend his good offices to secure the services of a tinker he knew by the name of Williamson who was prodigious on the chanter.

Then there were the total abstainers whom he pitied so long as they did not cross his path. He might sometimes talk of Hector Munro's public house as 'a little hell', but it was the beer to which he objected as something slushy and stupefying. 'A drop of spirits' he always esteemed as one of the mercies.

There were in his acquaintance, and in other ways high in his respect, certain rabid teetotalers, with whom he sometimes stayed on his excursions into the south. But in all these houses there was at least one understanding heart, and before he went to bed he would reach his hand into the darker corners in the bottom of the wardrobe.

Abstinence was a matter for the individual conscience. He would not have it imposed on others. He looked on unfermented wine as an abomination, though there were in the Free Church some ministers who subscribed to the innovation. He was assisting once at a Communion when he detected the substitution. This was a point in which he could never acquiesce. Putting the chalice away with the back of his hand, he said clearly, 'Take away that . . . that chelly.'

—— * ——

Uncle George had no telephone in the manse, but would have a strident shot at using it, in other houses and Post Offices, when necessary. When he did use it, he spoke only in English, under the conviction that the General Post Office, being a Sassenach institution, had not got round to adapting its electronic instruments to cope with the Gaelic — though there was, in his day, a Gaelic word for the telephone, which translated as 'the long whisperer'.

Aunt Maggie, believing that the Devil was in it, never spoke on the telephone at all, except at third hand. This involved the employment of a 'secure' intermediary to call the number and pass the questions and answers back and forth. When it came to the party line, Aunt Maggie's misgivings about security were only too well founded.

The party line was a great and entrancingly instructive institution which, I believe, survived longer in the Highlands and Islands than elsewhere. It was a service that had its own codes and conventions. No one ever complained about what they overheard; indeed if there was any complaint it was that the other subscribers were, if anything,

143

too reticent and cryptic in their conversation. It must have been inexpressibly tantalising to the eavesdropper on a piece of important local scandal suddenly to hear one of the callers go cautious, and hiss just at the best bit, 'Careful, ca-a-a-areful. Party line!'

There was also an ingenuous belief that you might secure privacy for your conversation by opening it with some such remark as, 'Hold on a minute; there is some low, inquisitive, poison-pen bugger of a busybody listening in.'

In the pause which followed it was usually possible to hear the faint click of up to half-a-dozen telephone receivers being replaced. The experienced user of the party-line, however, made the reassuring click, but with the same movement removed the telephone receiver again, in time to lose nothing of the ensuing conversation.

In Caithness during the War there was a characteristic security phenomenon, which was centred in Uncle George's native village of Lybster. The watching-posts of the Observer Corps, sited along the tops of the precipitous coast, were connected by the local telephone party-line to the headquarters filter room at Lybster. A circumstance, this, which meant that their observations were not confined to the look-out for possible German aircraft. There was even romance in the air.

There was at that time a namely and mature liaison, involving as it did a couple of local celebrities, in which the Caithness gossips were taking a fascinated interest. And although this, even after forty years, will probably be transparent to those in the know, I still feel that I must change the names a little. Here, then, is an authentic transcript of an operational Service exchange.

'Hullo, Lybster Centre. Post B-for-Beer calling.'

'This is Centre, B-for-Beer. Over.'

'B-for-Beer here. What's the meaning of the word "platonic"?'

'Centre here. I've no idea. Why in the world do you want to know?'

'B-for-Beer here. I've just heard Anaeas Sinclair using it to Maggie Fraser on the party line.'

'Centre here. Well, if it's Anaeas using it, then it's no' decent. Get on with your observing. Over.'

144

CHAPTER FIFTEEN

LEWIS AND MORE TRAVELLING OCCASIONS

SOME thirty years after Uncle George had left Stornoway for Fearn, I went to Lewis, a place of which I had heard much but seen nothing. And there I found his memory still green with the recollections of his journeys, his harangues, and his conversations. There was even a younger generation that knew him, and of him, for the Long Island had remained on his itinerary of communions and special services.

By that time, however, he was ageing, and his visits had become rare. But I was able to keep him in touch with a territory which in many ways, both physical and moral, had passed beyond his experience.

In 1942, having tholed my training at Cranwell as a radio-location operator, I was posted as an Aircraftman, second class, to the chain-home radar station at Bayble and Shader on the Eye Peninsula. And I found it possible to arrange things so that I could have a sentimental and avuncular session at the manse at three-monthly intervals.

This was simply a question of adjusting leave passes in a way which should be familiar to all old sweats. The geography and distances of Scotland are well-known to be *terra incognita* to all English-based authorities; a circumstance of which it would be excessively honest and foolish not to take advantage.

My official home destination was Glasgow; and the journey involved the long and often stormy crossing of the Minch; the dreary train journey from Kyle of Lochalsh to Inverness; and the change, there, to the south-bound main line. With the co-operation of a sympathetic orderly-room clerk, and by the discreet addition of the words 'via-Tain' to the travel warrant, it was possible — and by a well-practised avoidance of the Redcaps in Inverness station — to take the north train into Ross-shire. There were no inquisitive Service officials at Fearn station. And, after the short visit, to complete the journey to Glasgow, all I had to do was to take a train back to Inverness (still using the same travel warrant) and, if questioned there, maintain that I had just arrived from Kyle of Lochalsh. This procedure also worked just as well in the opposite direction. This break made no difference to the time I had at home— when I got there — because of the 'travelling time', an entitlement which, again with the contrivance of the Orderly clerk, we had worked out to a sliding scale of between 48 and 60 hours.

On these wartime visits to Uncle George there was always much to report. Island transport had always been, if not an obsession, at least a practical and intimate concern with him. I was therefore in full empathy with him when I reported that Henderson's horses, of foundering memory, had disappeared, but that they had been most worthily succeeded by the Lewis motor bus.

On this singular conveyance I was able to give an intimate progress report— in a special sense of that phrase. I knew, and learned to love it best on the final Saturday evening run from Stornoway to Garrabost, which was the airman's road-end for the RAF camp. This was no insensate mass of mechanism. It had character and a feeling for the island roads; and like the old vanman's horse, it knew itself the road-ends where it was expected to stop. Indeed the driver seldom took much to do with its direction. It did this very well on its own, leaving him to sit side-on in his seat with his head turned towards the passengers, an infinitely relaxed company, with whom he engaged in bi-lingual banter; and from time to time, in his role as master of ceremonies, leading and conducting the company in a few choruses of 'Ho-ro My Nut-brown Maiden'.

It was with a near sense of outrage that some time later in the Stornoway Gazette we, its patrons, read that the bus (or one of its siblings) had been made the subject of prosecution in Stornoway Sheriff Court, when its operator was fined £10 for letting it loose on the roads with no horn, no windscreen-wiper, no speedometer, no fire-extinguisher, no efficient handbrake, and no Road Fund licence.

It seemed hard that its intrinsic vivacity, and the good baurs and excellent singing of its jovial company could not have been cited in extenuation. The charges, taken in turn, were obviously irrelevant. No vehicle emitting the sounds that came from its passengers and its moving parts, had any need for a horn. Even in the usual wind-and-watery climate of Lewis, a windscreen-wiper was surely a luxury when the driver did not look through the windscreen. And what would they be doing with a speedometer when everyone knew that the bus had only one speed— full out— and that it took an hour from Stornoway to Tiumpan Head? That anything could take fire, or having taken fire could remain burning in the Lewis weather was too ridiculous to contemplate. Of what use was a handbrake when the driver was using both hands to illustrate the point of a good story? Finally, there was no use exhibiting the identification of a licence when everybody knew not only who owned the bus, but what his great-grandfather's nickname was— and when he was hoping to get another second-hand tyre for the off-front wheel, which had been giving trouble ever since it took away the milestone near Knock.

—— * ——

While I was in no position to brief Uncle George upon the spiritual state of his former parish— except that MacBrayne's steamer still did not sail on the Sabbath— I was adequately genned-up on the more material trivia, like the bus, and on the personal fortune of the people — a surprising number considering the passage of the years— who were eager to be remembered to him. My connections, of course, gave me immediate entry to the hospitality of the Free Church manse, a privilege I used discreetly, mainly while waiting for the midnight stroke that permitted the steamer to leave on the Monday morning for Kyle of Lochalsh.

This was the civilised funnel through which I introduced my new wife to the island way of life when she came north and west on a holiday visit to supplement the 48-hour honeymoon that was all the Service had vouchsafed us between my passing out at Cranwell and my posting to the Long Island as a radio-direction-finding clerk.

The same orderly clerk who fixed my travel warrants, arrranged my living-out-pass. We found a billet in a tiny croft overlooking the Broad Bay, where our aged landlady spoke only the Gaelic, and where my helpmeet was initiated, but without mastering it, into the art of cooking on a peat fire.

There were happily by that time other welcoming tables in the district to which I was in the habit of drawing up a chair. So peat-reek apart we did not all that badly, though it often meant two miles of stumbling through the mossy waters, slaps and stiles, and the deep dark waterlogged peatbanks to the repast.

So far as my wife is concerned, food, in the abstract, is an ineradicable memory of that time and in this the Free Church manse at Stornoway and the minister's wife have much relevance. The visit over, we had come down from the outpost by the ration truck to wait for the steamer, and for the hours of waiting until midnight we took refuge in the manse, where we were entertained, first with nourishment, and then with a wide-ranging conversation, which eventually found its way around to cookery. In this department the manse at Stornoway had had simple tastes — to the extent that the minister's wife seemed to have some sense of guilt about her possession of a special Lucullan book of banquets which she had received in a present. It is called *Recipes of All Nations*, its author the Countess Morphy, who sounds foreign, and may be famous, but who certainly knew her way around the *hautes cuisines* of both hemispheres.

The book is three inches thick, has some 800 pages, covers, as it claims, the exotic eating and drinking of all nations, with ingredients and instructions for their preparation, including the perfumes of Araby. With what looked like Calvinist relief, on one side, the book changed hands that night; and it lies before me, inscribed on the fly leaf, 'To Mrs Phillips, with best wishes, July 1942, C. MacRae.'

It was a kind thought, or it would have been in other circumstances, and there is no doubt that it is remembered for its feasts. At midnight I escorted my wife to the boat, saw her, as I thought, comfortably settled on board, and returned to my lonely vigil in the wilderness, and my night-watch supper of two slices of white bread sandwiching a half-inch-thick slab of dense and pallid issue cheese.

As for the better half, I must here recapitulate the main features of the war-time journey from Stornoway to Glasgow, not forgetting that that night there was a bit of a storm (which elsewhere but on the Minch would be classified as a hurricane). The crossing to Kyle of Lochalsh took seven hours; and this meant that there was no time to spare there, or at Inverness for the taking and changing of trains. In those days the trains ran slowly and with long unscheduled halts. So it was at least four hours from Kyle to Inverness, and five or six more

148

from Inverness to Glasgow. The station bookstalls were closed. There were neither canteen nor buffet cars on train or boat.

Forty years later that journey is relived again and again in this household, in all its parched and starved detail by its victim, who not only had nothing to eat or drink for some twenty hours; which might possibly have not been intolerable had she not had nothing at all to read but Countess Morphy, and the detail of such snacks as *Gans-Leber, Potchki V. Smetainie, Halkocsonya,* and *Pollitos Salteados* — to mention only a few out of a choice of many hundreds. With, of course, the indispensable wines to match.

—— * ——

From a very early age I was myself an experienced traveller on the north-country railway lines. On the day after the school closed for the summer holidays I would be taken to Buchanan Street Station, and, with my ticket tied to my button-hole, I would be put in charge of the guard of the train to Inverness.

Sometimes I would be met at Inverness by an uncle or an aunt and escorted the rest of the journey into Ross-shire or Caithness, but, as often I was just transferred from the care of one guard to the other. There were no risks about such travelling; there were no corridors to encourage irresponsible wandering; the door was usually locked; and at every station the bearded face of the guard which projected more authority than either parents or school teachers would appear at the window to check and perhaps encourage a little when it was plain that I had wearied of the comics (which in any case never held their interest beyond Perth). There were not even some of the more obvious discomforts, for, although there were no corridors, neither was there the need for hasty departures from the train and a scamper across the platform when it stopped at a station. Most of the third-class compartments were designed each with its own cubicle containing, with its other facility, the ingenious round steel, self-emptying tip-up wash basin.

There was entertainment, too, not excessive, but it was something reassuring and familiar over the years to know for a surety that when we came to Aviemore, there would be the same aged, tweed-clad musician parading up and down along the train playing his fiddle, and giving us the same repertoire from Scott Skinner and Neil Gow.

The railway guards, indeed, could be more reliable super-intendents of a small boy on a train than Uncle George himself. And I

have the thumb-nail on my right hand to prove it. It is noticeably wider than the corresponding nail on my left hand, and is my souvenir of one holiday journey when he was at Inverness to meet me. He certainly saw me well provided with fruit and sweetmeats, and a comic and a puzzle to hold my attention while he with two other clerical familiars got on with a discussion of the finding of the meeting which they had obviously been attending. During the stop at Dingwall he was engrossed in conversation when I carelessly left my thumb in the hinge of the open carriage door. Suffice it to say that when the whistle went a porter on the platform slammed the door. The accident, (it put a period to the post-mortem on the Synod meeting), did have its compensation in the days that followed later when the pain had subsided, and I became the object of flattering attention in the playground of Balmuchy School, where there were daily inspections while we watched the colours change from red, to blue, to black, and waited for the nail to fall off. And during that time, of course, I was excused the labour of writing on my slate.

Then there came a long-extended period when, first by myself, and later accompanied by one or other, or both of my own children, I took the night train from Glasgow; and this still sets me thinking gratefully of the Edwardian splendour, and gossipy attention of the dining car that, until not all that many years ago (and by that I mean something

between twenty-five and thirty) used to be coupled to the 6.40 am train to the North from Inverness. It stayed on always to the Mound, and sometimes to Helmsdale.

It was a high-set carriage of inlaid wood, and round mirrors, and leather armchairs that were anchored to the floor, with such a length of chain as gave plenty of latitude for the bulkier sorts of passenger to draw himself comfortably to the table on which he had such a breakfast as went out with Beeching.

The stewards were Highlandmen who had a higher regard for your appetite than for the catering profit of the company. You got country porridge, thick and lumpy, and if you asked for it you could have your milk in a bowl to set beside your place.

The plate was not taken away until you were asked if you needed more, but when you were initiated you declined, for it was wise to leave room for the kippers that were to follow, and then the bacon and eggs. Here one found no respect for a dainty appetite, for I remember, though it now sounds like a myth, the common invitation: 'Now are ye sure ye couldn't be doing with two eggs? We've got plenty.'

The tea and the toast and the marmalade and all the local news from the stewards were equally generous, and there was no haste, because in truth there was seldom more than one or two other passengers in the dining car.

My memory of the personal quality of the service is condensed in the picture, common to countless journeys, of the waiter, leaning on his knuckles on the other side of the table, and interrupting his conversation to lift the lid of the teapot and say, 'Ach, this is getting cold. Wait you till I get you another hot one.'

For the returning native this sort of thing gave you a cosy sense of belonging. And it was not confined to the railway. When I was Caithness bound in the years after the War (when Aunt Maggie was still alive), I disembarked at Helmsdale. My destination was Dunbeath, some twenty-five miles beyond the railway station, on the road to Wick.

I always expected to be met. But once when I came out of the station there was no car in sight; and as I was standing there, a little lost and saddened among my luggage, a bus drew into the station square.

I glanced at it without much interest. It had come in from somewhere south of Helmsdale. Then the conductress, a young woman whom I had never seen before, descended and walked straight towards me. I thought idly that she was probably hurrying in to collect a message from the booking office; but she stopped opposite me and said without further introduction, 'Your mither said to tell you that the doctor couldna come. I'm to take you hame on the bus.'

Thus taken charge of, I climbed on board, and if there was any lingering feeling that I might still be responsible for myself, it was removed a few minutes later when she came along with her ticket machine. But without any 'Fares please', she said instead: 'I'll just give ye a single. They'll surely manage to put ye back to the station. How long are ye home for?'

Nor did her interest and supervision end there. Uncle James's widow was then living in a house by the roadside a few miles over the Ord on the Caithness border. As we approached I looked out of the window in case somebody saw me, and I might be accused of not giving a wave in the passing. Aunt Johanna was in the garden, but she was walking away towards the door of the house.

As the bus carried on without stopping, I became aware of the conductress standing in the aisle beside me and bending down to look through the window over my shoulder. As she straightened up she said, her voice full of regret at what she took to herself to be a failure of the bus's personal service: 'What a peety. She's no' lookan.'

CHAPTER SIXTEEN

DISCRETIONS OF AUNT MAGGIE

AUNT MAGGIE always carried around with her a
homely atmosphere of conspiracy. She had a strong but elusive
character. She seldom argued, though she sometimes raged a little,
and she usually had her own way. When she came to Glasgow on a
visit she seemed to be helpless, with no sense of direction and a terror
of traffic. It was frightening to escort her, for she flinched at street
corners, and needed constantly to be reassured that we were on the
right tramcar. She was utterly dependent.

But sometimes she did have to venture into the streets on her own.
Then we would receive an anxious and solicitous telephone call,
perhaps from a manse in the farthest recess of Shawlands, and a voice
would say: 'Mrs Mackay has just left. She says she is going to try to
come out to you at Bearsden. I do hope she will be all right, but there
really was nobody here that we could send with her.'

The strange thing was that she would turn up almost immediately,
quite unflustered, and having made the trip in record time.

She usually arrived with a list of the old friends whom she intended
to visit, and sat back while a team of local relatives tried to trace them
from the addresses which she always just failed to remember exactly.

But she went to Australia with the maiden name of a school friend
who had emigrated thirty years before, either to New South Wales or
Queensland, she could not be sure which, and within three days of her

landing at Sydney she had not only found the married name and address but had made a journey to pay a surprise visit.

Although she spent a year there while Uncle George was taking the temporary charge of a Free Church Congregation in Sydney, Aunt Maggie never really believed in the existence of Australia. This was a typical achievement, for their adventures included being caught in a bush fire and a few meetings with the aborigines.

When they came home we interrogated her closely, but she had hardly noticed the fire and the black fellows had made no impression on her preoccupation with her search for cousins and Caithness folk.

'But,' we would ask, 'what did the place look like?'

'Well,' she replied, 'there were some places where the houses were painted in bright colours. But, you know, when you looked at them, maybe on a hillside in front of you, you just thought they were a frontage, with nothing behind them. But I must say the weather was good for your uncle's bronchitis.'

She also had an abject fear of the telephone and under no circumstances would she answer it. At the same time she never came south without a complicated social programme that called for a great deal of arrangement. This was made a little difficult because she was never willing to say exactly what she intended to do, and her instinct for avoiding any possible friction or pique was such that she would not dream of letting one of her acquaintances know that she intended to pay a call on another of them first.

Many of these engagements were made by telephone, which meant that one of Aunt Maggie's nephews made the call and acted as go-between, passing on the messages and possible times of arrival that were whispered to him as he stood with the receiver at his ear. Nor was it simply a matter of repeating the exact words of a Highland woman who had a superstitious dread of the instrument and would not touch it. The prudent essentials had to be extracted from such breathless instructions as:

'Say that I'll be coming out at three o'clock to-morrow afternoon, if I'm spared; but don't say that I've been down here since last Thursday; and ask how they all are, but don't mention Mary or John or Alec because I don't think they're speaking; and if they ask if I've been to see them don't tell a lie but just pretend you don't hear, and say that, yes, I'll be there at three o'clock.'

There were incoming calls as well that required the transmission of considered answers to casual questions.

And yet when left alone in the house for a couple of hours Aunt Maggie had an admirable capacity for subduing her fears and using the telephone to co-ordinate her visitations and bring her social news up to date with the efficiency of a business executive.

A similar reserve might be noticed in her attitude towards the wireless set, which she believed to be an invention of the Devil, designed, by broadcasting religious services, to keep the lax out of church, and then, taking advantage of the moral weakness it encouraged, to fill them with the light-mindedness of people like Stainless Stephen. She herself had not the remotest idea of how the controls worked or where the signals of any station might be picked up. In any event the electricity with which the set was operated was a desperately dangerous new-fangled thing and not to be tampered with. In addition, and perhaps most gravely, the wireless put an obstruction in the proper flow of gossip and conversation.

She shunned it, but she always could tell you the headlines of the news and the details of the weather forecast, and showed disingenuous talent for undetected wireless operating and listening that was unequalled outside a Japanese prisoner-of-war camp.

Aunt Maggie's circumspection was a personal refinement of the sound and independent Scottish principle that you should aye keep something to yersel', and was founded in the benevolent belief that what folk didn't know wouldn't hurt them. She had a confidential, and, indeed, a hypnotic way of saying, 'Now we'll chust do so and so.'

Her motives, though not always discernible, were of the best. She was wonderfully discreet, except when, in her direct way, which was always subtle, it suited her purpose to be direct. She had lived long enough in Easter Ross to know many personal histories, both romantic and piquant, but she would never give away just exactly who it was who, at last when hope seemed to be fading, was proposed to in the trap which was taking her to the railway station, nor whose trap it was she meant when she said: 'And when I saw it going back along the road past the manse with the trunk still tied on the back of it, I knew that he'd come to the point.'

Uncle George was himself incurious, and was content in the complete confidence he had in Aunt Maggie to handle all the worldly matters that were likely to come his way. He did not ask questions, and she protected him against the little indiscretions that might have disturbed him— such as the sewing on of a button on the Sabbath— with the simple and kindly warning: 'Now, don't tell your uncle.'

This was a reticence that occasionally touched him quite closely. He had a strong constitution and a stout heart, but throughout his life he was almost unremittingly harassed by bronchitis. He submitted to many treatments and at one period that which gave him the greatest relief was to have his back painted with iodine.

One evening when he was in great distress Aunt Maggie soothed him and applied the remedy, and he seemed to grow easier even as the first stroke passed across his shoulder blades. When he had been painted from the nape of the neck to the small of the back he sighed.

'My word, but that's much better,' and he lay down and fell at once into an easy sleep that carried him refreshed into the morning.

He never knew that when Aunt Maggie picked up the iodine bottle she had seen that it was empty, and had spent a generously deceitful half-hour painting his back with a dry brush.

CHAPTER SEVENTEEN

OLD AND MILD

W H E N I returned from the War there was a new librarian in the Glasgow Herald. He was older than I, and there was something vaguely and distantly familiar about him. But I could not place him. And for his part he looked at me knowingly too, but without comment. Then one day he fished out of his pocket-book a browned and fading snapshot print, and he handed it to me.

There was Aunt Maggie, her hair still jet black, seated with great dignity on a garden chair at the front of the Fearn manse. Uncle George was beside her, slimmer than I remember him and with more hair. At the back, also as yet unlined by the years, stood this colleague, whom I now recognised as a student preacher, and one of the few stickit ministers in the Wee Free Church. Squatted on the gravel at their feet was myself, six years old, fat, round-eyed, and solemn.

That was Uncle George in his vigour, whom I would remember, fit to hunt a heresy, or ready to steer the boat to Stornoway.

—— * ——

Age mellowed Uncle George and taught him a tolerance that he would have scorned to admit in his prime. It was the last time I saw him that he had just been persuaded by a fortunate and, I fear, jesuitical member of his flock that a win on the football pools was not gambling but the reward of skill and study and diligence, comparable with the prizes that he had himself won sixty years earlier in the bursary competition that was open to all the schools of Caithness.

If I had not seen it coming that would have been a sensational change in him, for I can remember the time when no one would have dared to argue with him. He would have stated his opinion and that would have been the law. But only a year or two earlier I had noticed that he was eloquent on the side of charity and a liberal interpretation of the evidence in an investigation into an alleged heresy on the part of one of the Free Church's lay preachers in the Presbytery of Dornoch.

He had in his day been stern and courageous in rebuking wrong, but by that time the role of prosecutor and judge had been assumed by some of the younger brethren, whose vehemence contained more than a hint of their regret that they had risen up in an age when the old discipline was declining and they were called to minister to a generation that was learning to answer back.

Uncle George had fallen into the habit, too, of not asking questions of his nearest and dearest when he knew that he must disapprove of the answer. It was a discreet accommodation that had its beginnings many years ago, when he used to come to Glasgow, but lived in our house only on week-days. Though the subject was never mentioned, he suspected that my father wrote the 'Man You Know' and drew his Bailie cartoons on Sunday afternoon and evening. But it was only toward the end that the indulgence was extended to myself, and when I went north to see him just before I was leaving the country in 1944, and only a few months before his death, he ignored the fact that to get there I had clearly travelled part of the way on the Sabbath.

———— * ————

He was in his 73rd year when he retired from the church at Fearn a little wounded in his spirit. He had taken a stroke which left him frail. For thirty-five years he had been training his congregation to acknowledge his vigour and to fear his catechising, and they saw the change in him before he was himself fully aware of it, or ready to admit it. He went away from them in sorrow and lived in Tain, where he listened to others preach, and he walked forlornly among his old friends and elders when they came into town on the market days.

Then he died, quietly and willingly, and, indeed, formally.

The last of his contemporaries who saw him was the old doctor whom he had known a lifetime. He came and they sat together and talked composedly for an hour alone, and then, when they had said all they had to say, they embraced one another and said 'Goodbye, in this world.'

The doctor wept as he came out into the hall; but Uncle George seemed settled in his mind and happier than he had been since he had left his church.

He died the next afternoon.